GOD'S DAILY INSIGHTS™
FOR MEN

HARVEST HOUSE PUBLISHERS
EUGENE, OREGON

Scripture versions used are listed on page 175.

Cover design by Garborg Design Works

Interior design by KUHN Design Group

Editorial development by Meadow's Edge Group LLC

The quote on page 124 is from C.S. Lewis, *The Weight of Glory and Other Addresses* (New York: Simon and Schuster, 1996), 26.

For bulk, special sales, or ministry purchases, please call 1 (800) 547-8979.
Email: Customerservice@hhpbooks.com

God's Daily Insights™ for Men
Copyright © 2022 by Meadow's Edge Group LLC
Published by Harvest House Publishers
Eugene, Oregon 97408
www.harvesthousepublishers.com

ISBN 978-0-7369-8127-9 (Milano Softone®)
ISBN 978-0-7369-8128-6 (eBook)

Library of Congress Control Number: 2021941644

Printed in China

21 22 23 24 25 26 27 28 29 / RDS / 10 9 8 7 6 5 4 3 2 1

INTRODUCTION

Do you have questions about God? If so, you're not alone. Most of us regularly ponder what God is planning or already has in the works for our lives. Many questions will not be answered until we meet Him face to face in eternity. Oftentimes the answers are not what we expect them to be. However, we do know some concrete truths about God because He's chosen to explain Himself through the Scriptures.

God's Daily Insights for Men was developed to help us have a better understanding of some of the questions that make us wonder what it is that God is doing in us. As you read through each devotion and Scripture, ask God to equip you and to help you take hold of the answers and establish them in your own heart. While you read, absorb, and embrace God's answers, take a moment to write down daily reflections and affirmations. Doing this will help you gain ownership of what you have just learned.

Through these readings, the hope is that you will be well on your way to discovering God's truths that lead to the faithfulness of His promises for your life.

NEW BEGINNINGS

God promised that He will transform us when we become part of His family. He will do a new thing in us, and He will continue to bring forth change that will be for our good and His highest glory.

God is able to make rivers spring forth in the desert. If He can do that, He can be trusted to cover the messes we made in our past—and supply everything we need for a bright, new future. That's the kind of God He is. He is the One who can take broken, worn-out, dusty, or failed experiences and plant a beautiful garden.

If we want to experience all that He has for us, we must begin with the simple belief that He loves us and wants to do something special in us—no matter what has transpired up to this very moment. One of the ways you show that belief is by seeking His will for your life, trusting Him for His wisdom to help you make right choices and go in the right direction.

Ready for a fresh start? A new start? Turn to God. You can trust Him to guide you to a brand-new beginning!

Forget the former things; do not dwell on the past.
See, I am doing a new thing! Now it springs up;
do you not perceive it? I am making a way in
the wilderness and streams in the wasteland.

Isaiah 43:18-19

PATIENTLY WAITING

Waiting is difficult—crawling behind a car that is going well below the speed limit in a no-passing zone, tapping your foot in line at the coffee shop as someone scrounges up exact change, anxiously waiting for the mailman so you can get your hands on that check that was promised weeks ago, and of course, trying to keep a great attitude in church on the very Sunday you planned to meet friends for lunch at 12:30 and your pastor decides to include next week's sermon in with this week's. Maybe the toughest waiting is when we ask God for direction on an important life decision.

No, waiting is not easy. But God tells us to wait patiently for Him—His choices, His answers, His news, His guidance, His perfect spouse for us, His desire for our vocation, His love, and yes, even His coming again. Waiting patiently means trusting God knows what is best for us because we are His children. God wants us to wait for Him because when we acknowledge Him in all our decisions, we truly begin to walk in wisdom.

Guide me in your truth and teach me,
for you are God my Savior,
and my hope is in you all day long.

PSALM 25:5

GOD'S STRENGTH

It's true that God is mighty, that He can do anything. And yet Scripture also tells us that God often uses humble means of exercising His power. In 2 Corinthians 4:7, Paul wrote that God can use imperfect people to do His will: "We have this treasure in earthen vessels, that the excellence of the power may be of God and not of us" (NKJV). And Jesus taught us that if we want to be great, we must serve. Philippians 2:7 tells us that Jesus Himself "made Himself of no reputation, taking the form of a bond-servant, and coming in the likeness of men" (NKJV).

So if you're feeling not-so-powerful or unsure of what contributions you can make, take heart. God in you is more powerful than you could ever be on your own, and He has prepared great things for you to do.

That is why, for Christ's sake, I delight in weaknesses,
in insults, in hardships, in persecutions, in difficulties.
For when I am weak, then I am strong.

2 CORINTHIANS 12:10

THE SECOND BIRTH

Think about it: You can be made new! Even if you have failed in business. Even if you have experienced broken relationships. Even if you turned your back on God and did exactly what you wanted to do—even though you knew those things were wrong.

Everyone living has experienced a natural birth. But just as Jesus promised Nicodemus in a late-night meeting (see John 3), we can also be reborn, born into the kingdom of God, becoming His children by spiritual rebirth. What a gift!

With this new status as children of God, we receive a new purpose, a new mission in life. In Matthew 28:19-20, Jesus told His disciples—and us—to take the good news of forgiveness and new beginnings throughout the world: to our own family and friends, to our next-door neighbors, to our coworkers, and to every other person we know and meet. We become ambassadors for Christ's message of new life, sharing this message of hope with a world that desperately needs hope!

If anyone is in Christ, the new creation has come: the old has gone, the new is here! All this is from God, who reconciled us to himself through Christ and gave us the ministry of reconciliation.

2 CORINTHIANS 5:17-18

IN THE BEGINNING

When we discuss the economy and new jobs, invariably entrepreneurs and small business owners are mentioned. Those brave souls who leave the security of an established company—and regular paycheck—to start a new venture.

We can admire men and women who dare a bold new beginning, but the ultimate Entrepreneur, the original Entrepreneur, the One who gave the most to accomplish the most is none other than God, the Creator of the universe and all that is. Now *that's* a business story, a love story, and a grand adventure rolled into one.

When was the last time you praised God the Creator? When was the last time you thanked God for creating *you*?

In the beginning God created the heavens and the earth.

Genesis 1:1

MAKING CHOICES

Lot faced a significant decision. He had the opportunity to choose which land to settle—land that would support his family and his flocks now and in the future. It was an important decision, so Lot looked around and surveyed the land carefully.

As lot's uncle, Abraham could have pulled rank and had the first pick. However, instead of carefully looking over the land, Abraham looked up to the Lord. Abraham's faith was in his unseen God. He did not make choices based on what looked most attractive to him, as Lot did. Instead, Abraham acted with confidence that God would not only guide him but also accompany him in whatever direction He led him to go.

What is the basis for your decisions? Although we need to consider the situation wisely, we must remember that appearances can be deceiving. When Lot chose the well-watered plain of Jordan, he also chose Sodom. Like Abraham, we must also look up to the Lord for His guidance when making choices.

Abraham said to Lot… "Is not the whole land before you? Let's part company. If you go to the left, I'll go to the right."

GENESIS 13:8-9

LEARNING TO WAIT FOR GOD'S BEST

Children can be impulsive and often want everything *right now*. (So can grownups!) Wise parents do not give in to every demand, but rather keep some things on hold until the time is right.

God deals with us the same way. He makes every good thing available to His children—but only in the right time. As our Father, He loves to prepare us for all that He has for us to know and enjoy. But out of fatherly wisdom, He trains us to trust Him—even when we want something right now—so we will become mature, Christlike adults who are better able to appreciate and enjoy His blessings. He also keeps us from greedy self-centeredness by answering some of our requests with a firm no.

To try to move ahead of God's perfect plan for us is to deny Him the privilege of teaching us and watching us grow to be like Him.

The Lord bestows favor and honor; no good thing
does he withhold from those whose walk is blameless.
Lord Almighty, blessed is the one who trusts in you.

Psalm 84:11-12

THE GREAT RACE

Life has often been compared to a race, and it is often a test of our will, our endurance, and our resilience in the same way a physical race is.

What's the secret of making it to the finish line? Is it determination? Is it trying harder? Is it mustering every ounce of courage we can find? Is it asking great people to help us? Those things all sound great, but we'll never make it to the finish line on our own efforts—even if others help us. In this way, the Christian race is different from a marathon or a mad sprint.

The Christian life has always been and will always be about trusting God and relying on His power and help, not just to bring us salvation, but to help us take each step of our life journey. That victorious finish will not come by trying harder—but by trusting Him more!

Commit to the LORD whatever you do,
and he will establish your plans.

PROVERBS 16:3

THE GOD OF THE LIVING

Skeptics hounded Jesus with questions and objections to His teachings and ministry. Some undoubtedly had honest questions to discuss. Others attempted to undermine Him by catching Him in an error.

A Sadducee—a teacher who didn't believe in the afterlife—tried to make Jesus look foolish by asking who a woman would be married to in heaven if her first husband died and she had taken a second husband (see Luke 20:27-39).

Jesus revealed the false assumptions behind the question, and then He made the bold proclamation that all that really matters is whether you—that Sadducee, the other listeners, and each of us reading His words today—have been made new and have personally experienced the power of the resurrection.

That doesn't happen through having devotions or being a good person. It's a miracle we can ask for and receive as a gift from God.

Have you been made alive?

He is not the God of the dead, but of the living,
for to him all are alive.

LUKE 20:38

CALLED AND ENABLED

Those whom God calls to a specific task, He always enables. The Lord knows when we have been faithful, and He gives us more—and His "more" will always stretch us. We would probably find it easier to continue being faithful right where we already are than go to the next level in our walk with God, but then we would stop growing. So God puts us in places of greater service than we have ever had before.

But along with every challenging call comes God's perfect enabling. He is prepared to meet every need we will face as we step out in obedience and faith. He will grant us the strength we need to match every demand. He will bestow the wisdom we need to navigate every decision.

It is an awesome experience to realize that Almighty God is personally equipping you to serve Him. If God is calling you to a new assignment, be encouraged—you are about to experience His empowerment like never before.

I thank Christ Jesus our Lord who has enabled me,
because He counted me faithful, putting me into the ministry.

1 TIMOTHY 1:12 NKJV

ON TOP OF THE WORLD

The highest peak in the country of Wales is affectionately called "the Top of the World." On a visit one summer, the wind blew and the clouds billowed, and all around as far as the eye could see were white spots—sheep dotting every pasture all the way to the lowest valley below. It was a breathtaking sight. No one on earth could create such a scene, not even the best set designer in all of Hollywood. Nothing compares to the intensity and exhilaration we feel when we are actually on top of a mountain.

We will experience mountaintop highs in life—and we will walk through some deep valleys as well. We can't always experience life on top of the world, but the mountaintop moments God grants us—spiritually and through the splendor of His world—will give us reminders of His love when we walk the inevitable valleys that are part of the human journey.

Take time to remember some of those special moments God has brought into your life and be ready to face anything with optimism, hope, and confidence!

Every good and perfect gift is from above,
coming down from the Father of the heavenly lights,
who does not change like shifting shadows.

JAMES 1:17

WHAT MAKES
THE DIFFERENCE

Do you already know what you need to do? Already feel a sense of purpose? Already have your eyes on a project or endeavor in your work? Your homelife? Your personal development? Your spiritual journey?

Do you already have something to accomplish but fear how you are going to get it done? Whether you will be successful? Whether you have the strength and abilities?

Good! You're in a wonderful place to get started. And there is only one place to start. Turn to God. Tell Him your fears. Tell Him you are not sure you have what it takes. Then ask Him to provide you with His strength, encouragement, and wisdom to get the task done.

Maybe you don't have what it takes. But God does. And that makes all the difference!

Look to the Lord and his strength;
seek his face always.

Psalm 105:4

TRUE CONFIDENCE

Confidence is…

- Diving off the high dive.

- Introducing yourself to someone new in a social gathering.

- Attending a workshop or seminar not because it's required at work, but just because.

- Visiting patients in a hospital—or prisoners in a jail—even though you've never met them before.

- Looking at someone who has told you about a difficulty he or she is experiencing and asking them, "Can I pray for you right now?"

Confidence means taking bold steps. And each of us can do just that, even if we don't consider ourselves to be very confident. Why? Because God is with us wherever we go.

Have I not commanded you? Be strong and courageous.
Do not be terrified; do not be discouraged, for the
LORD your God will be with you wherever you go.

JOSHUA 1:9

THE FUTURE IS BRIGHT

No one knows the future. Oh, some economists are better than others at predicting tomorrow's economic conditions. Some technology experts are better at predicting what tools we will be using in the days to come. Some sociologists are better at predicting societal changes and shifts that are ahead. But no one knows the future.

Except God. And He knows the plans He has for you. Some of which are greater and more exciting than you can imagine today.

Yes, we should plan appropriately for the future. But we aren't to think about the future with fear and anxiety.

What lies ahead? You already know the answer. With an open and obedient heart, great works and great moments God has planned specially, just for you!

> *What no eye has seen, what no ear has heard,*
> *and what no human mind has conceived…*
> *God has prepared for those who love him.*
>
> 1 Corinthians 2:9

A LIVING SACRIFICE

Ezekiel's ministry was marked by visions, prophecies, symbolic actions, and unpopular speeches. At times his actions appeared extreme: He set his face against a clay tablet (Ezekiel 4:1-2), lay on one side for 390 days and the other side for 40 days (4:4-6), shaved off his hair (5:1-4), and spoke of his many visions of judgment.

Under the triple burden of opposition, confusing circumstances, and an arduous assignment, Ezekiel remained faithful. He also knew that in the midst of adversity, people do not need a better understanding of their plight—they need a fresh vision of God's majesty and the reminder that no matter the crisis, God is sovereign.

Ezekiel's unique ministry exemplifies a life completely surrendered to God and committed to His purposes. The prophet serves as one of Scripture's most notable examples of being a living sacrifice in service to God. Ezekiel found his strength in the Lord, and we can too.

The word of the LORD came expressly to Ezekiel the priest...
and the hand of the LORD was upon him there.

EZEKIEL 1:3 NKJV

LIVE SMART

Some troubles come though we have done nothing to deserve them. An illness. An accident. A betrayal. An act of evil.

But other troubles run our way because we call for them through carelessness, questionable decisions, and sin.

In Psalm 90, David cataloged how hard life can be, how many woes befall us. He would know. He experienced troubles that were not of his own making, but he also experienced heartache and woe that he brought on himself. No wonder he encouraged us to number our days (verse 12). We are wise to heed the words of one who knows.

Are there thoughts or deeds in your life that are inviting trouble?

Teach us to number our days,
that we may gain a heart of wisdom.

PSALM 90:12

A NEW HEART

Near death, the word came through that a new heart was available. A young man was killed in a motorcycle accident. The older man had his transplant surgery that same week.

With the surgeries came a new life for him. He was suddenly healthier than he had been in years. He regained energy that had been drained. He was joyful and excited about life. And he understood the sacrifice that was made so that he could truly live again.

His comment: "As a Christian, this tragic and joyous experience made me more fully understand that God gave His only Son so I could have new life, not just here on earth but for eternity. I am grateful to God for the gift of life and the sacrifice that brought this to me."

God gives us new beginnings, but His very best gift of life is the one we will experience throughout eternity.

I will give you a new heart and put
a new spirit in you; I will remove from you your
heart of stone and give you a heart of flesh.

Ezekiel 36:26

PAUSING AT THE CROSS

Our thoughts are far from being God's thoughts. We strive to serve our lives; God commands us to give our lives away. We want to exalt ourselves; God instructs us to humble ourselves. We aim to be first; God tells us to be last. We adamantly defend ourselves; Jesus asks us to turn the other cheek. We cannot think like the world does yet have the mind of Christ. We must allow the Holy Spirit to transform our carnal, self-centered, ungodly thinking.

Consider whether you are adopting the mind of Christ—His willingness to serve, His passion to be obedient to God to the point of death, His unblemished holiness. Do you truly want to have the mind of Christ? Are you willing to abandon your current values, prejudices, resentments, jealousies, and unforgiveness? Are you prepared for the Holy Spirit to expose those areas of your thinking that are not in line with Christ's?

May pausing at the cross remove the pride that defines God's right to your life and keeps Him from using you for His glory. It is incredibly freeing to think like Jesus.

Let this mind be in you which was also in Christ Jesus.

PHILIPPIANS 2:3 NKJV

CONTENDING FOR FAITH

The Greek word "contend" means "to earnestly struggle for something." It suggests striving against opposition as if in a battle. It's a contestant striving for victory against a foe. Jude exhorts Christians to "contend…for the faith" (Jude 3 NKJV) as combatants in a spiritual conflict.

After all, evil forces seek to rob us of our faith and disrupt our relationship with Jesus. Christ's adversary will do whatever is in his power to destroy the body of Christ—and this reality ought to keep us alert. We can't afford to have a casual Christian faith. Rather, we need to guard it and nurture it. We need to fight for it.

In what ways are the Christian faith in general and your faith in particular being attacked today? More importantly, what are you doing to stand strong? Don't forget to put on the armor of God—the belt of truth, the breastplate of righteousness, the gospel of peace, the shield of faith, the helmet of salvation, and the sword of the Spirit (Ephesians 6:13-18).

I found it necessary to write to you exhorting
you to contend earnestly for the faith which
was once for all delivered to the saints.

JUDE 3 NKJV

A BOLD MOVE

The easiest step and the hardest step is the first step. Is something keeping you from getting started? Are you holding on to a self-destructive attitude or habit that deep down you want to be rid of?

- Someone you won't forgive?
- A temptation you run toward rather than away from?
- An area of your life that is weak and needs strengthening?
- A sin from your past that calls for restitution?

Is it laziness? Is it procrastination? Is it stubborn pride? Is it a sense of defeat before you even start?

Today is your day. It won't be easy, but you can succeed with God's help. Today is the day to take the first step.

Let us run with perseverance the race marked out for us.

Hebrews 12:1

TURNAROUND

Is it fair to say we live in a lax, permissive, indulgent age? That doesn't include everybody, of course, but many of us put pleasure before discipline in our own habits, in our child-rearing, and in our attitudes toward the behavior of others.

Part of this prevailing attitude is due to our desire not to be judgmental. That is a good impulse. But some of it comes from being too comfortable in our relative wealth and easy lifestyle!

Repentance is turning away from sin and going in an opposite direction. Not all our choices deal with sin, but nevertheless, the wise person incorporates discipline and even self-denial to grow toward maturity.

In what ways do you need more discipline in your life?

Unless you repent, you too will all perish.

LUKE 13:3

GOD STILL SPEAKS

Throughout the Bible, God interacts intently, intimately with those who seek after Him. He whispered to the prophet Samuel as a young boy. He spoke directly to and through the prophets. He wrestled with Jacob. He called David a man after His own heart and greeted Mary as someone "highly favored." And in Jesus He walked among us, just as He did with Adam and Eve in the Garden of Eden.

Thousands of years later, God is still speaking. He longs to hear from us, His children, in prayer, and He wants to speak back to us. Relationships thrive on communication—regular, quality communication. Through prayer and listening to God through His Word, we can experience a loving, thriving relationship with none other than God Himself.

My sheep listen to my voice;
I know them, and they follow me.

John 10:27

YOU'VE BEEN SENT

Moses was raised and educated in Pharaoh's court as a young nobleman. But when God called him to lead his people from slavery, he was terrified. He was afraid to speak, much less lead. He had good excuses. He stuttered. He had a criminal past. He had been abandoned by his mother as a baby.

But then he saw God in a burning bush. One by one his excuses were stripped away. His doubts and questions were answered as only God can answer. And he, a refugee far from home, was sent with a message from God.

You've been sent too. With a message from God. No excuses. No giving in to fear. Are you ready to say yes?

> Moses said to God, "Suppose I go to the Israelites and say to them, 'The God of your fathers has sent me to you,' and they ask me, 'What is his name?' Then what shall I tell them?" God said to Moses, "I AM WHO I AM. This is what you are to say to the Israelites: 'I AM has sent me to you.'"
>
> EXODUS 3:13-14

GOD'S ANOINTED

We live in an immoral and evil world. Our society is filled with voices inviting us to turn away from God and to pursue the carnal world's values. We must be alert in this kind of environment.

Thankfully, God has given us all we need to stand strong in His truth and His ways. He has given us His Word as our guide and our foundation. Scripture clearly sets forth God's truth, His commandments, and His instruction. We do not have to be confused in this complicated and deceptive world.

God has also given us the church. Believers are not to stand alone. We are called to be iron sharpening iron, to bear one another's burdens, to hold one another accountable for decisions and choices, to go to one another for counsel and prayer. We don't have to face the enemy on our own.

You have an anointing from the Holy One.

1 John 2:20

DISCIPLINE YOURSELF
FOR TOUGH LOVE

Solomon, the wisest man who ever lived, told his son not to be resentful because of God's discipline. He said that a father's discipline is a sign of love. Perhaps Solomon was thinking about his own childhood. His father, King David, was a mighty warrior—but was also known to be somewhat indulgent with his children. Maybe Solomon was reflecting on whether a firmer hand of parental discipline would have benefited him in his own life!

You can discipline yourself, or you can leave it to someone else to do it for you. Even if a boss, parent, spouse, friend, or customer won't step up and hold us accountable for our decisions, the good news is we have a heavenly Father who cares too much about our actions and the state of our hearts to just ignore things we do wrong. That's His tough love.

Have you experienced God's chastening? Guard your heart from resentment and receive God's discipline for what it is—a sign of His love.

My son, do not despise the LORD's discipline,
and do not resent his rebuke, because the LORD disciplines
those he loves, as a father the son he delights in.

PROVERBS 3:11-12

THE WAY OF FAITH

When mountain climbers are in dangerous terrain, they rope themselves together. Sometimes one of them slips or falls. But not everyone falls at once, and so those who are still on their feet are able to keep the unbalanced climber from falling away completely. And of course, in any group of climbers, there is a veteran climber in the lead.

The letter to the Hebrews identifies Jesus as our lead—the One who both began and finished this race we're in.

Traveling in the way of faith and climbing the ascent to Christ may be difficult, but it is not worrisome. The weather may be adverse, but it is never fatal. We may slip and stumble and at times even slide a few steps backward, but the rope will hold us. We can have complete confidence in God's firm grip on our lives. Even if we slip or fall, He is there to catch us and secure us for the climb ahead.

> *… looking unto Jesus, the author and finisher of our faith,*
> *who for the joy that was set before Him endured the cross,*
> *despising the shame, and has sat down at*
> *the right hand of the throne of God.*

> HEBREWS 12:2 NKJV

POSSIBILITIES

The Bible spends only a few pages establishing the conditions of our beginnings. The next several hundred pages cultivate in us a taste for the future—immersing us in a narrative in which the future is always impinging on the present.

The future is not a blank to be filled in, depending on our mood, by either fantasy or horror, but a source of brightness that we await and receive. Our lives are still outstanding. Our prayers give expression to lives that go far beyond the past and present and reach into what is promised and prophesied.

When we pray, we realize that our true identity is not who we are or have been—we understand ourselves in terms of possibilities yet to be realized.

The sufferings of this present time are not worthy to be compared with the glory which shall be revealed in us.

ROMANS 8:18 NKJV

GOD ACCOMPLISHES GOOD

We cannot afford to be naive about evil. Rather we must face it without being intimidated by it. It will be used by God to bring good. One of the most extraordinary aspects of the good news is that God uses bad men to accomplish His good purposes.

If we forget that the newspapers are footnotes to Scripture and not the other way around, we may become afraid to get out of bed in the morning! Many of us spend too much time reading just the headlines and the editorial page, which often focus on the negative.

Journalists provide helpful information about politics, economics, and other world events. But the deeper meaning behind the activities we see in the world is most accurately given to us by God's Word—the only truly good news we can always rely on.

Show me Your ways, O Lord;
teach me Your paths.

Psalm 25:4 nkjv

REMEMBER GOD'S GLORY

What is your faith story? At what moments has God's grace been unmistakably at work in your life? What stories of His deliverance have you heard and embraced for your life?

Knowing your Christian heritage can strengthen your trust in and devotion to God. Passing your faith along to your family members is a privilege and a duty. God commands His people to remember His mighty deeds.

The Israelites were to tell the next generation about the powerful works God did in delivering them from slavery in Egypt—the plagues, the angel of death, the parting of the Red Sea, and the destruction of the Egyptian army. Likewise, we are to tell the next generation about the wonders God performed when delivering us from slavery to sin—Christ coming in human form, living a sinless life. His willingness to submit to death on a cross, the brutal crucifixion, the glorious resurrection.

It is crucial that we pass along to our family our own stories of life with God. Let's not let unbelief rob our legacy of faith.

You shall tell your son in that day, saying,
"This is done because of what the LORD did
for me when I came up from Egypt."

EXODUS 13:8 NKJV

WALKING IN THE SPIRIT

Walking in the Spirit is a choice we make. It involves choosing—moment by moment—to live under the direction and in the power of the Holy Spirit.

Walking in the flesh will always produce sin. Walking in the Spirit will always result in righteousness. Life situations are opportunities for the Spirit residing in us to live out His life through us and to reveal to a watching world what God is like.

To open yourself to the work of the Spirit, linger before the cross of Jesus Christ. Gaze at the cross until sin's grip loosens and Christ's love takes hold of you. After all, the crucifixion and resurrection were the pivotal events that ushered God's power into our lives. In the Holy Spirit—by His power—you can know His strength, and you can reflect His divine character in any circumstance.

Walk in the Spirit, and you shall not fulfill the lust of the flesh.

GALATIANS 5:16 NKJV

HUMBLE STRENGTH

Victory is indeed a fleeting experience—and that may be especially true of spiritual victories. You may have held your tongue (victory!), but it won't be long before another rude comment comes your way (tempted?). Or you may have controlled your temper (victory!), but the next spark could soon ignite a rage (temptation). Thinking about how well you did in a situation—as opposed to giving thanks for the Spirit's help—makes you prideful and an easy target for failure.

While you're busy celebrating a success, the enemy can catch you off guard and bring you plummeting down. So praise God for your success. Focusing on Him like that will keep you from letting pride suggest that you're invincible. You are always in critical need of God's strength and guidance—but especially right after a victory. Turning to Him, especially after victory, will keep you from falling.

Let him who thinks he stands take heed lest he fall.

1 Corinthians 10:12 nkjv

A LOVING TOUCH

For many of us, God is more an idea, a principle, a concept, a distant thought than He is a Person. A real, live, feeling Person.

No wonder we forget that God loves us not in principle, but with feeling! Think back to childhood—to climbing up on your father's lap and experiencing the strength and warmth of his arms as he held you and read to you or asked about your day at school. Even if that wasn't your exact experience, you get the picture. How lovely to know that our heavenly Father cares that much.

There are many stories throughout the Gospels about people being touched by the Lord: Jesus feeding the five thousand, Jesus healing a man who was paralyzed, Jesus raising Jairus's daughter from her deathbed, Jesus reaching out to heal the leper, and Jesus healing the blind man are just a few. The examples of Him reaching out and touching people demonstrate His personality and passion. And He continues to extend His touch to His children in a multitude of ways today.

Our God isn't an abstract principle—He is definitely a "hands-on" God!

Moved with compassion, Jesus reached out and touched him.

MARK 1:41 NLT

HIS TERMS, NOT OURS

When your heart is far from God, His ways will seem puzzling and His guidance less important. When your heart is far from God, His voice will be muted, and His Word—if you even read it—will seem strange.

You might think, *God is always there for me*—but don't presume upon Him. Our sin distances us from our holy God, and it may keep us from finding Him in times of distress. As the nation of Israel had to learn the hard way, God is available to us on His terms, not ours. We may presume on God's presence, but that does not mean He will "be there" for us like we thought.

So go to Him on His terms. Return humbly and with a pure and contrite heart, with a willingness to both learn from Him and to serve Him, with an openness to being filled by Him and used by Him. You'll see that the more you revere the Lord, the more Christlike you become, the more you will understand God's ways, and the more readily you will follow Him.

With their flocks and herds they shall go to seek the LORD,
but they will not find Him; He has
withdrawn Himself from them.

HOSEA 5:6 NKJV

FOR GOD SO LOVED YOU

Very few people question that God is loving. But many of these very same people question whether God truly loves them—or ever could. They are certain God hears the prayers of others, forgives others, has plans for others, is patient and loving with others—but not for them.

How about you? Do you know that God not only loves the world, but also loves you? Personally. On a first-name basis.

One simple activity that might make that point crystal clear to you is to write out John 3:16, but in place of the word "world" insert your own name. For God so loved [your name]. Then read the verse out loud several times today—and tomorrow. In fact, you might try that right now.

Your life will change when you experience for yourself the reality that God loves the world and every individual in it—and that most certainly includes you.

For God so loved the world that he gave his one and only Son,
that whoever believes in him shall not perish but have eternal life.

JOHN 3:16

A SURE FOUNDATION

During the Great Depression, many people lost hope in the government, their churches, their families, and even God as the downward spiral of economic disaster engulfed everything they owned. People who had previously been considered upper middle class found themselves standing in soup lines. Those who had ordered their lives around money faced dismal futures, and suicides became common.

Sound familiar? Is it possible that living in a prosperous society tempts us to put our hope in the wrong things?

The truth is that no earthly thing deserves our trust. Recent economic woes and front-page scandals demonstrate once again that even the most stable institution, person, or system can fail. But when we place our hope in God, we find His protection and renewal even in the deepest valleys of our lives on earth. He alone is a worthy foundation on which to build our lives.

Those who trust in the LORD are like Mount Zion,
which cannot be shaken but endures forever.

PSALM 125:1

SEEKING THE LORD

You've probably spent time looking for something you knew had to be in the house or in the garage or maybe in the office. You know, for instance, that you used your keys to drive home—they have to be around here somewhere! It is extremely frustrating to look for something that refuses to be found, isn't it?

In Scripture, the word "seek" does not mean searching for something hidden or lost. Instead, to seek is to come to something—someone—who is familiar to you and who wants to be found by you.

Despite God's passionate desire that we come to Him and experience Him, we must approach Him on His terms and on His timetable. So today, seek the Lord with energy and enthusiasm, for you will find Him!

Seek the Lord while He may be found,
call upon Him while He is near.

Isaiah 55:6 NKJV

A COURAGEOUS HOPE

What keeps us from attempting—let alone accomplishing—great things? None other than fear! No wonder the phrase "fear not" is found more than 100 times throughout the Bible. The opposite of fear is courage. But how do you get courage if you're afraid?

The psalmist tells us that there is something we can do to build our courage: hope in the Lord (Psalm 31:24). There's no other starting point. It's the only thing that enabled David to face Goliath (1 Samuel 17:1-51), Gideon to lead a small ragtag army against the mighty Midianites (Judges 6:1–7:25), Joshua to cross the Jordan River and later conquer Jericho (Joshua 3:1-17), Peter to walk on water (Matthew 14:22-29). And it's the only thing that enables you and me to face any giants and challenges that come our way.

Is your hope in God?

Be of good courage, and He shall strengthen your heart,
all you who hope in the LORD.

PSALM 31:24 NKJV

SERVING GOD

God's desire is for us to do what is on His heart and His mind, and Samuel did just that. Samuel chose to serve God, not himself.

Samuel's name, meaning "heard by God" or "appointed by God," signified his birth as a direct answer to prayer. For years his mother, Hannah, had longingly prayed for a child. Dedicated to the Lord before his birth, Samuel lived as a Nazarite, never forsaking his mother's vow that he would serve the Lord all his life. He functioned as a prophet, an intercessor, a priest, and the last of the judges. He helped Israel make the transition from a theocracy led by judges to a monarchy ruled by kings.

Clearly fearing God more than he feared men, Samuel often spoke stern and condemning words of truth about the actions of powerful leaders such as Saul and David. Samuel's life also exemplified the foundational teaching that "to obey is better than sacrifice" (1 Samuel 15:22)

Today, ask the Lord to give you a heart to obey Him and the desire to do what is on His heart and His mind.

I will raise up for Myself a faithful priest who shall do
according to what is in My heart and in My mind.

1 Samuel 2:35 nkjv

STRENGTH IN THE LORD

David knew well what it was like to both walk obediently with God and also to fail to obey His commandments. When David trusted in God, giants fell, opposing armies were routed, and enemies were defeated. Many of David's psalms record his joy in God's love and protection on his life.

But David also grievously disobeyed his Lord and suffered the painful consequences. Some of David's most heart-wrenching psalms record his grief over the devastating consequences of his sin against God—and David lived daily with the consequences of his sin. He therefore earnestly desired that his son Solomon not make the devastating mistakes he had made. David recognized that only by carefully keeping God's commandments could Solomon enjoy the abundant blessings God wanted to give him.

Take time to research the Scriptures for God's commandments and instructions. They are far too important for you to remain unaware of any of them.

Be strong, therefore, and prove yourself a man. And keep the charge of the LORD your God: to walk in His ways, to keep His statues, His commandments, His judgments, and His testimonies.

1 KINGS 2:2-3 NKJV

A PATTERN FOR LIFE

Before we can move ahead for God, we must withdraw from the usual activities of life and be with Him. The more meaningful those times of retreat are, the more significant our times of spiritual advance will be.

This was clearly Jesus's pattern for life. Prayer was not incidental to His kingdom work—it was the foundation and the lifeblood of what He did during His ministry.

When Jesus prayed, He was not merely looking to have the Father endorse His plans. Rather He was seeking His Father's will. We must do likewise, for there is too much at stake for us to miss God's will. We want to join God in the work He is already doing in the world. It's too easy, in our zeal for God, to rush into plans and ministries for Him that actually oppose His purposes. God does not need our ideas, our initiative, or our imagination. He already has a plan. He is simply looking for our obedience.

[Jesus] often withdrew into the wilderness and prayed.

LUKE 5:16 NKJV

THE LORD WILL PROVIDE

The instruction was strange, unsettling, incredible. Abraham was to sacrifice his long-awaited son, the boy through whom the Lord was to fulfill His promise to bless the world (Genesis 22:2).

Abraham obeyed. He gathered the wood, picked up his knife, and carried fire with him for the sacrifice. He built the altar, laid his son on it, and lifted his knife. Then the angel of the Lord called to him, telling him not to lay his hand on Isaac. Abraham's actions up to this point showed the Lord the degree of his faith, and He provided another offering for Abraham's sacrifice.

The Hebrew name for Jehovah Jireh means "The Lord Will Provide." This name speaks of the completeness of God's care for Abraham in particular and for His people for eternity. Just as God provided a ram as a substitute for Isaac, He would provide a Savior as a substitute for all people. Praise God for providing for you—day by day and for eternity.

Abraham lifted his eyes and looked, and there behind him was a ram caught in a thicket by its horns. So Abraham went and took the ram, and offered it up for a burnt offering instead of his son. And Abraham called the name of the place, The-LORD-Will-Provide.

GENESIS 22:13-14 NKJV

ON WHOSE AUTHORITY?

The New Testament term "authority" means "freedom of choice." The greater the authority, the more autonomy one has to choose and to act. God has absolute sovereignty and is therefore completely free to do as He pleases. Once a divine decision is made, He cannot be thwarted by any power in the universe.

God—who has the absolute power to do whatever He chooses to carry out His will—has given His Son all authority, and the Son in turn gives power to those He chooses to represent Him. As His ambassadors, we Christians have Jesus's support for what we do for Him. This is a God-given privilege, not a license to do as we please. We are free not to do as we want, but to act according to the Lord's will.

Furthermore, the work of God's kingdom rests on Christ's supremacy, not our ability. Do not grow discouraged if a situation exceeds your competence and resources. At issue is your belief. Do you trust that Christ is able and willing to use your life to accomplish His work? When God sets an assignment before you, what you do next reveals what you believe about Him.

All authority has been given to Me in heaven and on earth.

Matthew 18:18 NKJV

FISH IN WATER

We're like fish in water when it comes to our sins. Some of our sins are so much a part of us that we don't even recognize them as sin, just as a fish doesn't acknowledge the water that comprises its world. When our sin fades into the backdrop, it is all the more dangerous in its subtlety. Just because we have grown accustomed to our sin does not make it any less loathsome to God.

God sees our sin. He knows what lies within the innermost recesses of our hearts. He is aware of our every thought whether or not we verbalize it. The psalmist knew he must deal with these issues—the thoughts of his heart as well as the words of his mouth prompted by those thoughts. And the psalmist knew he needed the Lord's help to do so.

God's help is available to you too. Turn to Him. Let Him cleanse you from your "errors" and "secret faults" and make your words and thoughts acceptable in His sight.

Who can understand his errors? Cleanse me from secret faults...
Let the words of my mouth and the meditations of my heart be
acceptable in Your sight, O LORD, my strength and my Redeemer.

PSALM 19:12,14 NKJV

HEAVEN, OUR GLORIOUS HOPE

Death is not the end for Christians. Oh, no doubt, it is still a time of sharp loss, acute pain, and a throbbing ache that lingers for years and sometimes a lifetime. Perhaps there is no greater sorrow than what is felt over the death of a child.

But woven into the heartache, there is a glorious hope for all who know God and have been redeemed by the blood of Jesus Christ. Death is not the final chapter of life, but rather a doorway into an eternity with God, where every longing of the human spirit is met and fulfilled.

Heaven is a place of no more tears. Death truly is different for God's children.

He will wipe every tear from their eyes.
There will be no more death or mourning or crying or pain,
for the old order of things has passed away.

REVELATION 21:4

PRAYING SCRIPTURE

James, the brother of Jesus, wrote, "The effective, fervent prayer of a righteous man avails much" (5:16 NKJV). When we face hard times, prayer can sustain us like nothing else—both the prayers of others and the continual prayers we offer for our own situation.

Perhaps one of the most effective ways to pray powerfully is to pray the words of Scripture. Just as Jesus responded to temptation with Scripture, so we can experience spiritual victory with the Word of God.

Pray God's promises and ask for their fulfillment in your life. Pray that those close to you would follow God's path for them. Pray for His kingdom to come, His will to be done on earth as it is in heaven. There can be no better words of comfort, strength, healing, love, and hope than the very words and thoughts of God as revealed in His Word.

*I pray also that the eyes of your heart may be enlightened
in order that you may know the hope to which he has called you,
the riches of his glorious inheritance in the saints.*

EPHESIANS 1:18

INVISIBLE REALITY

How can you prove God is real?

The truth is, even though there are wonderful arguments for the existence of God, you cannot prove His existence. You can point to His world and His works, but He is invisible. Some have heard Him speak in an audible voice, but again, no one has caught God on an audio recorder.

Is this a problem? Is it troubling? Not at all! If God could be seen through a telescope or under a microscope, would He be the Almighty God proclaimed in His Word? He's the Creator and as such cannot be studied in the same way as His creation.

Paul asked, "Who hopes for what they already have?" He also wrote, "Hope that is seen is no hope at all." Hope is for the deeper, more profound realities that require open hearts and eyes.

Hope that is seen is no hope at all. Who hopes
for what they already have? But if we hope for
what we do not yet have, we wait for it patiently.

ROMANS 8:24-25

THE VALUE OF HARD WORK

Scripture tells us to rely on God and to wait for Him. It tells us that He has blessings for us we can't earn and that He loves to give gifts to His children.

But there's another principle in the Bible that we shouldn't ignore: the principle of hard work. The book of Proverbs instructs us to look to the ant, who has no "overseer or ruler, yet it stores its provisions in summer and gathers its food at harvest" (6:7-8). If we want a bright future—if we want to enjoy benefits in the short-term as well as the long-term—we have to put our nose to the grindstone and do some work.

So while it's important to wait on God and look to Him for provision, perhaps one of the best things to do while we're waiting is to work hard.

The plans of the diligent lead to profit.

PROVERBS 21:5

A SHARED HOPE

Church attendance is down in America. Fewer people attend, and those who attend do so less often. A number of reasons are given, including these:

- There are more Sunday morning activities than ever before.

- The church is no longer relevant.

- America is a post-Christian nation.

- Young people are not becoming Christians.

Whether you agree or disagree with these reasons, one thing is certain: The writer to the Hebrews said that meeting together is essential for the spiritual vitality of believers. He warns that living the Christian life is not easy, and we need to encourage one another and spur one another on to good deeds.

Do you have a weekly place where you meet with other believers for spiritual growth and encouragement?

Let us consider how we may spur one another on toward love and good deeds, not giving up meeting together, as some are in the habit of doing, but encouraging one another— and all the more as you see the Day approaching.

HEBREWS 10:24-25

THE SECRET OF LIFE

Mysteries and lost codes have never been more popular than in today's entertainment culture. Prophecies, cryptic clues, secret societies, dangerous searches, untapped divine power, buried treasures—all the components of an entertaining thriller.

The world Paul preached to was similar. There was a fascination with mysteries that unlocked godlike power and riches for humans inquisitive enough to solve the difficult and arcane riddles.

Paul wasn't a man to keep a powerful secret for just a few select individuals, to be hidden and protected from the masses. Instead he revealed the identity of the mystery that had eluded humans for generations: Jesus. The mystery solved is Jesus inside your life.

Have you experienced the glory and power of God inside you? You don't even have to search for God. He will find you!

> *… the mystery that has been kept hidden for*
> *ages and generations, but is now disclosed to the*
> *Lord's people. To them God has chosen to make known*
> *among the Gentiles the glorious riches of this mystery,*
> *which is Christ in you, the hope of glory.*
>
> Colossians 1:26-27

THE RIGHT ARMOR

God sees us in our need, saves us from our sins, and puts us on the right path. Our life changes for the better. We are thankful. But sometimes we get proud. And we begin to feel self-sufficient. And we forget that God is the One who turned our lives around in the first place. We make a mess of things. But God sees us, hears our call for help, redeems us, and puts us on solid ground again. And oftentimes, again.

Rather than live in a cycle of defeat, wouldn't it be better to remember—to never forget—that God is the source of our salvation and strength?

Are you facing life with your own sufficiency? Or are you wearing His armor?

> *Since we belong to the day, let us be sober,*
> *putting on faith and love as a breastplate,*
> *and the hope of salvation as a helmet.*
>
> 1 Thessalonians 5:8

NO WORRIES

Some people believe that worrying is a sin. Do you believe that? How could such a natural and common emotion be a violation of God's will?

Without attempting to answer that question, all of us can argue that worry is rarely, if ever, helpful—and it is usually detrimental to our quality of life. Worry is bad for our physical health, bad for our mental health, and it doesn't change anything.

Fundamentally, worry is a lack of faith in God and His protection and provision in our lives. That's why some call it a sin. It is true He doesn't promise to make everything turn out like we want it to. But He does promise to meet all our needs and to never forsake us.

Will you believe Him? If so, why worry? With God beside us, there are no real worries.

Are not two sparrows sold for a penny? Yet not one of them
will fall to the ground outside your Father's care.
And even the very hairs of your head are all numbered.
So don't be afraid; you are worth more than many sparrows.

MATTHEW 10:29-31

A DELAYED HOPE

When you were a child or teen, did you ever hope for something with seemingly all of your heart—but it never came to pass?

Even when it comes to temporal desires, Solomon said that "hope deferred makes the heart sick, but a longing fulfilled is a tree of life" (Proverbs 13:12). How are we supposed to handle the grown-up disappointment of having noble and spiritually motivated hopes delayed and deferred?

In Hebrews 11, we find a hall of fame of faith. Some received what they were promised, while others didn't—at least not here on earth. And therein lies the secret of maintaining a positive and optimistic sense of hope and expectation when things don't appear to be working out. It's the realization that in eternity, all hope is realized.

These were all commended for their faith,
yet none of them received what had been promised,
since God had planned something better for us so that
only together with us would they be made perfect.

HEBREWS 11:39-40

A RENEWED STRENGTH

In a world that can wear us down mentally, physically, and spiritually, how do we renew our strength? What do we do in the face of too many projects, too many temptations, too many conflicts, and too many other soul- and energy-sapping dynamics at work in life?

Others might help you. That's wonderful. But don't put your hope in them. You might be able to muster some more determination to get the job done. That's wonderful too. But don't even place your hope in yourself. The only place to turn for a renewed spirit is the One who has given you every good and perfect gift, including any strength or talent you were born with. What a wonderful promise that we can run without growing weary!

So how is your day? How has your week been going? How does this month look to be shaping up for you? Are you hopeful and inspired? Or are you discouraged? Either way, place your hope in the Lord and let Him give you a supernatural strength.

Those who hope in the LORD will renew their strength.
They will soar on wings like eagles; they will run and
not grow weary, they will walk and not be faint.

ISAIAH 40:31

HOPE OUT LOUD

People sometimes ask, "What's wrong with the world today?" Wars, worldwide strife, death and sickness, natural disasters—ours is truly a hurting world. Is it worse now than ever? That's another topic of conversation and debate! But one thing for certain has not changed in the course of history: the fallen human race needs God.

Perhaps that's why Peter instructed his fellow disciples to be ready to explain the hope they had. Knowing—and articulating—that it's God who saves us and gives us hope for the future is good for our own spiritual life. Sharing—articulating—that reason for hope with others offers them what they need to hear and is, again, good for our own souls. Are you able to verbally express the reason you live with hope?

The hope that is in us is not passive—it must be active in order to be effective. Nurture it within yourself, and be ready and able to proclaim it to everyone you know.

In your hearts revere Christ as Lord. Always be
prepared to give an answer to everyone who asks you
to give the reason for the hope that you have.
But do this with gentleness and respect.

1 PETER 3:15

TOO BUSY TO WORRY

The act of hope is so much more enjoyable than the act of worrying. And yet it's often so much easier to mull over our worries than to think about the hope God offers us.

An anonymous quote declares: "Blessed is the person who is too busy to worry in the daytime, and too sleepy to worry at night."

Maybe if we busy our minds with meditating on the goodness of God and how we can serve Him, we'll have less mental energy to worry.

Reading the Psalms, making a list of God's works in our own lives, singing along to a favorite worship song, serving others as a volunteer—there are all kinds of ways to spend our time that cultivate faith in God's promises and keep us from brooding over what may or may not happen.

Set your minds on things above, not on earthly things.

COLOSSIANS 3:2

NEVER FEAR

The fear reaction is wired into our brains, a part of our physiology. It's what triggers our fight-or-flight reaction, which can save our lives during sudden life-threatening circumstances. But fear is also an emotion that can interrupt our spiritual progress—and our lives in general—when it slips out of our control.

John, Jesus's "beloved disciple," contrasts fear and love in 1 John 4:18—the two are complete opposites. And if God is love, He is the solution to out-of-control fear. Whatever you're afraid of, surrender that fear to a loving relationship with God. If you're afraid of the past, remember that He makes all things new. If you dread the future, meditate on His providence and plans for you. If you fear the loss of relationship, remember that He will never leave you, and ask Him to help you nurture love and closeness with those around you. If you fear dying or losing someone, remember that He has conquered death.

Fear can be a formidable foe. But God is truly able to help us expel it from our lives.

So do not fear, for I am with you; do not be dismayed,
for I am your God. I will strengthen you and help you;
I will uphold you with my righteous right hand.

Isaiah 41:10

THE MIRACLE

Herman Ostry's barn floor was under twenty-nine inches of water after a flood. He needed a miracle—and fast—to salvage his barn and be ready for winter. He needed to move his entire 17,000-pound barn to a new foundation more than 143 feet away. His son, Mike, devised a lattice work of steel tubing. He nailed, bolted, and welded the lattice on the inside and the outside of the barn, with hundreds of handles attached.

After one practice lift, 344 volunteers slowly walked the barn up a slight incline, each supporting less than fifty pounds. In just three minutes, the barn was on its new foundation. And Herman had his miracle.

If you're holding out for a miracle today, don't be surprised if the one God sends you comes at the hands of your friends and neighbors. We can always count on Him to come through, but He very often uses those nearest to us to see us through a difficult time.

God is our refuge and strength,
an ever-present help in trouble.

Psalm 46:1

TO THE END

You haven't run a marathon until you cross the finish line 26.2 miles from the start. You haven't really read a new novel until you turn the last page. You aren't actually married until you exchange vows and the minister declares you husband and wife. You aren't an inventor until you dust off the blueprints you sketched on the back of a napkin and build something.

Throughout the Bible, one of the key themes is finishing strong. Paul ran the race of life to win—even though it meant martyrdom. He was not alone. Of the original apostles, only John died of natural causes. But even he was exiled because of his faith.

Are you as good at finishing as you are at starting? Not every endeavor we start requires our follow-through. Some things don't matter that much. But faith is not one of them.

We may never face physical persecution for our Lord's sake, but each one of us has been called to walk with God, not just for a season, but for all our days. Look to God for hope and strength on your spiritual journey.

God is not unjust; he will not forget your work and the love you have shown him as you have helped his people and continue to help them. We want each of you to show this same diligence to the very end, so that what you hope for may be fully realized.

HEBREWS 6:10-11

WALKING WITH PETER

Okay, he ended up sinking like a rock, but for just a moment Peter did something amazing. He walked on water.

Consider Peter's circumstances. When he left the boat, he was not in calm, shallow water on a beautiful, sunny afternoon. No, he was in the middle of a storm.

Some argue an act like that takes stupidity. But really it takes confidence. Not just a loud, self-aggrandizing, boastful kind of confidence, but the kind that truly believes a miracle is going to happen. For Peter, that belief was centered on Jesus. He had seen what He had done before and he trusted He would do it again in his life.

How is your sense of trust? Are you ready to walk on water when the next storm comes?

Peter got down out of the boat, walked on the water and came toward Jesus.

MATTHEW 14:29

HOPE CHANGES LIVES

A self-made millionaire, Eugene Land, forever changed the lives of a sixth-grade class in East Harlem through a simple act of hope. Mr. Land had been asked to speak to a class of fifty-nine sixth-graders. Scrapping his prepared notes, he decided to speak to them from his heart.

"Stay in school," he admonished, "and I'll help pay the college tuition for every one of you." Now that's a speech! And it had an impact for years to come. In a time and place when few students graduated from high school, nearly 90 percent of that class went on to attend and graduate from college!

Hope is powerful. When we cultivate hope and share it with others, we create a brighter future for them and us. Hope truly changes lives.

Through him you believe in God, who raised him from the dead and glorified him, and so your faith and hope are in God.

1 PETER 1:21

GOD HEARS OUR PRAYERS

A farmer who lived near London during World War II wrote to the Scripture Gift Mission requesting prayer that no bombs would fall on his small farm. He enclosed a five-shilling offering. He explained that his harvest had been awful, and he didn't have enough money to bring in water for the parched crops. He could not afford another setback without losing his farm. The secretary of the mission wrote back and said he could not ask that his farm be spared but instead would pray that God's will would be done.

Soon afterward the largest bomb in the German arsenal hit the man's farm. The impact was so big that it unearthed a spring. The spring not only amply watered his farm, but also enabled him to share water with his neighbors. And the next year, he enjoyed an abundant harvest. He sent a fifty-pound check to the mission as a thanksgiving offering.

Thank God for unexpected blessings.

Rejoice always; pray continually; give thanks in all circumstances; for this is God's will for you in Christ Jesus.

1 THESSALONIANS 5:16-18

I LOVE A RAINY DAY

When you have an outdoor wedding or a big family-reunion picnic planned, a rainy day feels like a disaster. But most of the time, there are lots of reasons to love rainy days!

- No mowing the lawn or washing the car.
- Outdoor events are canceled, easing a too-busy schedule.
- It's a great time to stay inside and read a book.
- The grass grows thick and green before the onset of summer heat.
- Newly planted flowers need the water.
- Flowers help us appreciate bright, sunny days.
- We might get to see a rainbow—a sign of God's faithfulness.

Rainy days. They may or may not be your favorite. But like all other days, they offer something positive. And since all days are God's days, a blessing can always be found in a storm cloud!

I have set my rainbow in the clouds, and it will be
the sign of the covenant between me and the earth.

Genesis 9:13

GAME DAY

Athletes love to compete. Nothing beats game day—a brisk fall evening of football, a hot summer day of baseball, a basketball or volleyball game in a packed field house where the winds of winter are forgotten. Game days are what you work for, what you live for as an athlete.

But practice? That's a different matter for many of these same athletes. What enormous, beefy football lineman wants to run sprints—better known as "gassers"—on a sizzling August day? What basketball player wants to lift weights in May? What soccer player wants to do sit-ups and planks in December until his or her stomach muscles are quivering? And yet training provides the strength, speed, and agility for a successful game day.

Life is filled with challenges. Some are the training ground in life to build our strength and character so we can face whatever comes our way. Other storms are more like hurricanes: They are the game days of life. They represent the moments when all our training and knowledge are put to the test.

Physical training is of some value, but godliness
has value for all things, holding promise for
both the present life and the life to come.

1 TIMOTHY 4:8

IN THE DAY OF TROUBLE

The shepherd boy who wrote and played music that touched the hearts of many had grown into a mighty warrior. He was Saul's beloved champion in battle—and yet the disturbed king burned with jealousy and rage at David's exploits.

He needed and wanted David close, but uncontrollable fits would overcome Saul and he would strike out to slay him. David's life was not safe. He lived in a state of vigilant fear, wondering what mood the king would be in at a particular moment.

But even in these unreliable circumstances, David believed God's hand of mercy and protection was on his life—that God would "hide me" or "set me high upon a rock" (Psalm 27:5) Few of us live in such an insecure state as David did. But we have troubles of our own. How is your faith?

In the day of trouble he will keep me safe in his dwelling;
he will hide me in the shelter of his tabernacle
and set me high upon a rock.

PSALM 27:5

PRESSED, BUT NOT CRUSHED

Abeloved husband and father died from cancer after years of chemotherapy and radiation, suffering in horrible ways from the effects of both. During that time, he clung to 2 Corinthians 4:8-10 as a source of hope. He prayed the passage constantly and found that it gave him courage to trust and endure.

He was perplexed, but not in despair. He was not forsaken and not destroyed, because he knew that come what may, the result would be the same: He would be with Jesus and experience the full and glorious manifestation of all His promises! His peace and poise under pressure became the touchstone for his family's faith after he was gone.

The good news is that we, too, can experience that hope. No matter what you are facing, God will preserve you and give you strength.

We are hard pressed on every side, but not crushed;
perplexed, but not in despair; persecuted, but not abandoned;
struck down, but not destroyed. We always carry around
in our body the death of Jesus, so that the life
of Jesus may also be revealed in our body.

2 Corinthians 4:8-10

WHEN A STORM
ISN'T REALLY A STORM

The following words may be upsetting to some. They may feel callous and insensitive. And they may not apply to your feelings and situations, but perhaps they are exactly what you—and all of us—need to read.

Here it is in a nutshell: Not all the things that we think are problems are really problems.

We live in a prosperous time when even the "poor" are often wealthier than those who are considered wealthy in another culture. We've become so accustomed to having so much that what once felt like a special blessing now feels like a necessity. Again, this does not apply to all areas of discontent, and it does not mean that demands for fairness are selfish and indulgent. But many of us need to do a reality check on what we think we need to be happy.

How about you? Are you more demanding than giving? Have you turned blessings into necessities? Have you moaned and complained over things that really aren't that big of a deal in the grand scheme of life? Maybe the trouble is not God's goodness but our ability to receive the gifts He gives us.

Praise the LORD, O my soul,
and forget not all his benefits.

PSALM 103:2

PEACE WITH MYSELF

Some people don't need to fight with anyone to be at war. Their battles are with themselves.

Maybe it was a tough upbringing. Maybe it was a traumatic event. Maybe it was a lost opportunity or relationship. Or maybe their battles within are the result of exalted opinions of themselves.

On this earth, few of us will ever be 100 percent satisfied with who we are and be totally at peace within. As we grow older, we should naturally experience that peace to a greater degree. But when self-warring is strong enough to hinder all other relationships, we need to take a good look inside.

Are you at peace with God? Do you believe He made you the way you are for a purpose? Your answers will lead you to how you need to pray!

We have different gifts,
according to the grace given to each of us.

ROMANS 12:6

FAITHFULNESS IN THE PIT

In Genesis 39:1-23, we read the fascinating story of Joseph. This handsome, proud, brilliant, favorite son—he had everything going for him—in an instant lost it all. He was unfairly sold into slavery by his own brothers and became a servant of Potiphar, an Egyptian army commander. Potiphar was so impressed with Joseph that he entrusted all that he had to Joseph's care. But just when things were looking up, Potiphar's wife made things much worse. When Joseph rejected her advances, she took revenge by accusing Joseph of trying to rape her. Predictably, Potiphar had Joseph thrown in jail.

But because Joseph was a man who loved the Lord faithfully, God blessed him even in the pit of prison, and Joseph was soon put in charge of all the other prisoners. Many years and events later, Joseph was made a ruler in Egypt.

If there ever was a person who had reason to rage against life's unfairness, it was him. But he was a man with so much faith in God that he conducted himself with a sense of peace and purpose even while living in the pit.

He remembered us in our low estate…
and freed us from our enemies. His love endures forever.

PSALM 136:23-24

ALL THINGS!

Our culture craves comfort, the avoidance of pain, easy projects, nothing but success, leisure time, entertainment, fun hobbies, and anything else that can fit under the umbrella of "smooth sailing."

When things don't go right—a conflict with a loved one, a demanding and troublesome boss, a leaky roof, car trouble, financial setbacks—there is a prevailing attitude of surprised anger and resentment, a strong sense that life is unfair and cruel.

Paul, a survivor of every sort of calamity, challenges this mindset. Not only are difficulties inevitable, but they become opportunities to grow—and even become catalysts for great things to happen. Are you convinced that all things work together for good in your life?

Accept discipline. Ask God to help you get the most out of the difficulties you encounter. You might feel pain for a moment, but the long-term rewards will be great.

We know that in all things God works for the good of those who love him, who have been called according to his purpose.

ROMANS 8:28

THE BURDEN BEARER

God tells us that He will bear our burdens, making our yoke easy. It is a promise to His children. But in order to experience His rest, we must first give our burdens over to Him. We do that through prayer, confessing that we cannot carry the weight of life without Him. He wants to bear our burdens for us and make our load light—but only with our permission.

There will be many people in our lives who will offer to carry our burdens. And while they can share in our pain and suffering—and while God often uses others as a means of His grace—people really cannot carry our heaviest burdens for us. They can help, but only Christ can lift the load.

Are you carrying a burden today that is best placed in God's hands?

My yoke is easy and my burden is light.

Matthew 11:30

SELF-INFLICTED STORMS

Life can feel very unfair—but it can feel very fair, too, even in the midst of storms. Not every calamity that comes our way is an accident of nature or a trial God has allowed to help us grow. Some storms are self-inflicted:

- Health problems after years of bad eating habits.
- Broken relationships after infidelity or a pattern of cruelty.
- Financial woes after overspending for years.

Those are storms—but they aren't unfair. But there's still good news. God is a God of second chances. He won't eliminate every consequence of dumb behavior, but He will give us new meaning and purpose in life when we return to Him.

Is there someone in your life who needs to hear again that God gives second chances? If it's you, will you receive His mercy today?

Before I was afflicted I went astray,
but now I obey your word...
It was good for me to be afflicted
so that I might learn your decrees.

Psalm 119:67,71

WHY WORRY?

In Matthew 6, Jesus told a parable expressing that the lilies of the field and the birds of the air are not concerned about where their food or clothing come from. They are clothed in beauty and eat plenty, even though they do not sow or reap. They have everything they need to live as flowers and birds.

We are to trust God so much that acquiring the daily necessities of life does not feel like a burden to us. Since God is great enough to create all that we can see—as well as the vastness of what we cannot see, then He is surely able to provide, as He promised, all that we need to sustain us in life. Now, if you are stewing because you don't have as much as your neighbor, but have a full stomach, that is another matter to deal with on another day.

But be assured, God will provide you with everything you need. So why worry?

Seek first his kingdom and his righteousness,
and all these things will be given to you as well.

Matthew 6:33

A HOPELESS HOPE

Abraham is known as the father of our faith. That title didn't come easily! First of all, he left his home in a sophisticated and affluent part of the world because he heard God calling him to a new land. Throughout his story in Genesis, the one constant is that he "picked up his tent stakes" and moved on.

But that was just the beginning of his challenges. When he got to the land, it was filled with warring tribes. Even harder to deal with, he and his wife seemingly could not have children. How do you become the father of a nation when you have no land and no child? But Abraham never gave up—and at an old age received his reward.

Will your faith persevere when you see no immediate results to feed your hope?

Against all hope, Abraham in hope believed
and so became the father of many nations, just as
it had been said to him, "So shall your offspring be."

ROMANS 4:18

THE MASTER
POTTER AT WORK

The potter must remake his vessels when there is a flaw in the clay that will cause it to crack later or when the color smears and he cannot get it to blend perfectly. He knows his craft, and he knows when to take it down from his wheel—to start over to remake it into a fine vessel that will appeal to customers and serve the one who buys it.

In the same way, God knows us intimately—He did create us, after all—and knows how to shape us into who He created us to be. He uses different ways, often tests and trials, to make us more like Jesus. The process is lengthy and often painful, but we will be amazed by God's handiwork in the long run if we simply submit to His loving hand.

*"Go down to the potter's house, and there I will give you
my message." So I went down to the potter's house, and I
saw him working at the wheel. But the pot he was shaping
from the clay was marred in his hands; so the potter formed
it into another pot, shaping it as seemed best to him.*

JEREMIAH 18:2-4

WORST-CASE SCENARIO

Many of Jesus's disciples were fisherman, and they knew from experience that the Sea of Galilee was notorious for its sudden storms. The squall recorded in Matthew 8:23-27 was especially furious. As the high winds whipped up the sea into vicious waves, the disciples grew frightened and frantic.

While all this was happening, Jesus was sleeping calmly in the back of the boat. The disciples finally had to wake Him because they were certain they were about to drown! Jesus woke up calmly and told the storm to be still. And it obeyed Him. He then looked at His disciples and asked why they had such little faith! They were simply speechless.

What did Jesus know that they didn't know? Ultimately, He understood the true worst-case scenarios in life are death and an eternity without God. He also knew that His work on the cross would deliver us from these worst-case scenarios. Anything else life throws at us is a snap compared to these. No wonder He was at peace. And that's exactly how we can experience peace in the midst of storms.

He replied, "You of little faith, why are you so afraid?"
Then he got up and rebuked the winds and the waves,
and it was completely calm.

MATTHEW 8:26

A WHALE OF A STORM

He was a faithful prophet of God, full of zeal and integrity. He knew right from wrong. That's why God's call for him to preach to the godless people of Nineveh caught him off guard. He may have had zeal and honor, but compassion and love weren't part of his spirit. So in a fit of anger and rebellion, he disobeyed God and went the opposite direction of Nineveh.

But God was intent that Jonah would follow His command, and He sent a storm and a fish to get him going in the right direction. (See Jonah 1:1-17.)

Amazingly, Jonah's preaching saved a people from destruction—though it never seemed to instill love in his own heart.

The next time a storm forms around you, it just may be an opportunity for you to do something bold for God on behalf of others. After all, those who have survived the storm can bless and help others who are in a storm of their own.

Whoever finds his life will lose it, and
whoever loses his life for my sake will find it.

MATTHEW 10:39

HOLD YOURSELF ACCOUNTABLE

When you think of experiencing peace in your life, you probably don't think of words like "discipline" and "accountability." But think again. When you lack discipline in your life, when you don't hold yourself accountable, what results? Usually chaos and problems. In other words, the opposite characteristics of peace.

If you want to experience peace in all its forms, it always begins with God's grace. But on that foundation, God has laid out a framework of plans and decisions within which we can live according to His will. They always require effort in the form of discipline and accountability. But what sounds like it could be a burden becomes a source of great satisfaction and reward.

Great peace have they who love your law,
and nothing can make them stumble.

PSALM 119:165

YOU ARE FORGIVEN,
AND I LOVE YOU

Several years ago in Spain, a father named Juan had become estranged from his son, Paco. After more than a year spent apart, Juan set off to find his son. He searched for months to no avail.

In a last, desperate effort to find him, the father put a full-page ad in a Madrid newspaper. It read: *Dear Paco, meet me in front of this newspaper office at noon on Saturday. You are forgiven, and I love you. Your father.*

On Saturday, eight hundred young men named Paco showed up, all seeking forgiveness and love from their fathers.

Our world is hungry for reconciliation. The good news is that a message of acceptance and forgiveness, an offer of peace, can go a long way. With whom can you share God's acceptance today?

"Come now, let us reason together," says the LORD.
"Though your sins are like scarlet, they shall be as white as snow;
though they are red like crimson, they shall become like wool."

ISAIAH 1:18 ESV

JUST ANOTHER NIGHT

On the night before Nicholas Ridley's execution in 1555, just hours before he was to become a martyr for his faith, his brother offered to remain with him in the prison chamber to help comfort him. But Nicholas declined the offer and replied that he intended to go to bed and sleep the same as he would on any other night of his life. Even his accusers were amazed at his peace and calm.

Ridley was undoubtedly well versed on the life of Paul. The man who took Christianity to the world wrote a letter to the Philippian church that became known as the "epistle of joy"—even though it was written from a prison cell as he was en route to Rome to face his death.

Our lives may not be threatened for the faith we hold dear, but we are still promised a supernatural peace when we lay down our heads at night, resting in the everlasting arms of God.

For to me, to live is Christ and to die is gain.

PHILIPPIANS 1:21

BE THANKFUL

Which comes first—the gift or the spirit of thanksgiving? Common wisdom says we get the gift first, then we say thank you for receiving it. While that is true, some gifts will never be recognized or received without a spirit of thanksgiving.

How many people sabotage the blessings in their life because of a crummy attitude? They are dissatisfied and disappointed—and let the world know it—despite a plethora of gifts from God and others all around them.

All of us can be thankful for the many things God has done for us. But there may be deeper levels of spirituality—even more of His nature and goodness—that we can experience through the attitude of gratitude. Have you said thank you to God today?

Let the peace of Christ rule in your hearts,
since as members of one body you were
called to peace. And be thankful.

COLOSSIANS 3:15

THE DOOR OF HOPE

Think about it. If you had everything you wanted, if there were no challenges in your life, if you didn't have any questions about why things are the way they are, and if you didn't feel there was something for you to accomplish that is bigger than your abilities—what would you have to hope for? Nothing, of course. You would already have everything.

We know that's not the way the world works—but sometimes we act and feel as though that's exactly what we believe. We seem surprised by problems and challenges.

We live in a fallen world with fallen people. That accounts for so many of the trials we face. But beyond that, God wants us to live in reliance on Him. For that reason, He doesn't grant our every wish and give us everything our heart desires exactly when we want it. He wants us to grow in the ways that really matter—patience, kindness, self-control, and other attributes of the fruit of the Spirit (see Galatians 5:22-23 for a list).

Don't have everything you want right now? Well, that gives you something to hope for!

Never be lacking in zeal, but keep your spiritual
fervor, serving the Lord. Be joyful in hope,
patient in affliction, faithful in prayer.

ROMANS 12:11-12

AN INVITATION TO PEACE

Peace is one of those elusive states of mind that run from us when we chase them. We can't get peace because it is our chief goal. Peace is almost always the result of other decisions we make in life: kindness, forgiveness, sober judgment, and many others.

If we want to experience peace, then there is no better place to start than pursuing the One who is the giver of peace, the Prince of Peace, the One whose sacrifice made peace between God and man—as well as man and man—possible in the first place. If you would pursue peace, pursue Jesus. Talk to Him. Listen to Him. Worship Him. Thank Him. Realize He is right beside you, and within you, closer than any human being could ever be to you. Experience peace by experiencing Jesus every day of your life!

I will listen to what God the LORD says;
he promises peace to his people, his faithful servants.

PSALM 85:8

BE OF GOOD CHEER

D on't worry, be happy" may be too simplistic of a formula for life, but the "be happy" part is definitely a principle from God's Word.

David said: "You have filled my heart with more joy than when grain and new wine abound" (Psalm 4:7 BSB). Solomon said: "A cheerful heart is good medicine, but a crushed spirit dries up the bones" (Proverbs 17:22). Jesus said: "In the world you will have tribulation; but be of good cheer, I have overcome the world" (John 16:33 NKJV).

Even if you have some problems and worries that are gnawing at you today, all the more reason to make a conscious decision to shake off the blues and embrace a cheerful disposition.

I have told you these things, so that in me
you may have peace. In this world you will have trouble.
But take heart! I have overcome the world.

JOHN 16:33

PURSUE UNITY

Churches, companies, families, charities, and other groups of people have split apart over the simplest and deepest disagreements. Something as crazy as the color of new carpet in the sanctuary has led some people to leave a church fellowship. To a church situated in the diverse and contentious city of ancient Corinth, Paul wrote with instructions to the believers to be of one mind and live in peace. If they pursued unity, he explained, they would experience God's peace.

We, too, live in a diverse and discordant culture. Civility has become the exception, not the rule. Rudeness is not only tolerated, it is sometimes applauded. This condition permeates politics, news, and entertainment—and encroaches into every area of community, including church and family.

Are you a peacemaker? Do your words and actions pursue a path of peace? If not, today is a new day to get started.

Strive for full restoration, encourage one another, be of one mind, live in peace. And the God of love and peace will be with you.

2 Corinthians 13:11

THE PATHS OF WISDOM

If asked, "How wise are you?" most of us wouldn't know exactly how to answer. We talk a lot about intelligence, but not very much about wisdom, so we don't always know what wisdom looks like. Solomon shared one sign that helps us recognize wisdom in our own life and in the lives of others when he described it by saying, "Her ways are pleasant ways, and all her paths are peace" (Proverbs 3:17).

Nobody's life is always and only pleasant. No one walks exclusively on paths of peace. Not even our Lord, Jesus Christ, experienced such a life, and He was the wisest man who ever lived.

But there can still be great insight gained by asking ourselves, "Do my decisions, attitudes, words, and lifestyle create peace or discord?" How we answer might suggest something about our current state of wisdom—and how we can become wiser in this world with God's help.

> *Blessed are those who find wisdom, those who*
> *gain understanding, for she is more profitable*
> *than silver and yields better returns than gold....*
> *Her ways are pleasant ways, and all her paths are peace.*
>
> Proverbs 3:13-14,17

THE PROMISE OF PEACE

Jesus's own life was anything but peaceful. He was born in a stable after an arduous journey. His family was forced to flee to Egypt when He was an infant because a madman was murdering baby boys. His father died. He became the most celebrated teacher of His country, drawing the wrath of the religious and political establishment. Ultimately, He died on the cross.

But Jesus brought peace—between God and man, between estranged family members, and even between enemies.

Why don't we see more evidence of it? As long as humans have the freedom to live for or against God, we will not see peace in full bloom. But the seed is planted. Sprigs and shoots can be seen in the most unlikely places. The promise of what is to fully be!

If it is possible, as much as depends on you,
live at peace with everyone.

Romans 12:18

THE GOD OF ALL COMFORT

Too much comfort can be a problem, obviously. Too much convenience, too little discipline can cause us to grow complacent, ineffective, unready for challenges that come our way. But there's a different, more necessary type of comfort—the kind of loving care that makes life not only bearable, but joyful. And the Bible tells us that God offers us that kind of comfort in abundance. Paul called God the "Father of compassion and the God of all comfort" (2 Corinthians 1:3), and David said of the Good Shepherd, "Your rod and your staff, they comfort me" (Psalm 23:4).

It's not that God is cushiony and coddling. It's that He has entered our world and taken on our pain. Even if He doesn't take away our hard times, He promises to stay beside us, loving us every step of the way.

And that is a very comforting thought.

[He] comforts us in all our troubles,
so that we can comfort those in any trouble
with the comfort we ourselves receive from God.

2 Corinthians 1:4

CHANGING NAMES

He was educated at the highest levels in both law and theology. He was an international traveler, aware and sophisticated in the ways of the world. A young leader with all the right connections, he was climbing the career ladder at a rapid pace. Devout. Respected. Even feared. But he was a man at war with himself. He was Saul.

On his way to Damascus, a trip where he planned to strike a violent blow against this new branch of the Jewish faith that was spreading like wildfire, he encountered the risen Christ. He was struck blind and Jesus spoke to him in an audible voice: "Saul! Saul! Why do you persecute me?" (Acts 22:7).

From that moment, the persecutor became a preacher. The man who was roiling inside with turmoil came to inner peace. Meeting the risen Lord changes everything!

Then Saul, who was also called Paul,
filled with the Holy Spirit...

Acts 13:9

IT IS WELL WITH MY SOUL

In 1873, Horacio Spafford sent his family ahead of him to Europe, planning to join them later. But the ship carrying his wife and four daughters never made it to the UK. After a collision with another ship, it sank, and Spafford's four daughters with it. His wife survived. Spafford took a ship to France to meet his wife, and when the ship passed over the site of the shipwreck, the captain showed him the spot where his daughters lost their lives. As he stood weeping on the bridge of the ship, God led him to write the words to the classic hymn, "It Is Well with My Soul." The opening lines still provide comfort today: "When peace like a river attendeth my way, when sorrow like sea billows roll, whatever my lot, Thou hast taught me to say, it is well, it is well with my soul."

Grief and heartache are real. But even in the middle of tragedy, when we accept God's will and loving care, we can experience perfect peace.

> The LORD gives strength to his people;
> the LORD blesses his people with peace.
>
> PSALM 29:11

PEACE IN MY HEART

You can do everything right and still not feel at peace in your heart about your relationship with God. In the eighteenth century, John Wesley came to America as a missionary, ministered to prisoners, and preached throughout the English countryside in open-air revival services. He read his Bible and prayed every day. But despite all those efforts, he still felt insecure and unsure of his salvation.

Then one evening, while listening to Luther's preface to the epistle to the Romans, Wesley saw that God alone can assure us of our relationship with Him. Wesley later wrote, "While he was describing the change which God works in the heart through faith in Christ, I felt my heart strangely warmed. I felt I did trust in Christ, Christ alone for salvation; and an assurance was given me that He had taken away my sins, even mine, and saved me from the law of sin and death."

If you're lacking assurance, turn to Christ alone, and your heart, too, can be "strangely warmed."

Let us draw near to God with a sincere heart and with the full assurance that brings faith, having our hearts sprinkled to cleanse us from a guilty conscience and having our bodies washed with pure water.

HEBREWS 10:22

THE WRITTEN
WORD OF GOD

Some Bible teachers have suggested that we should read the Bible each time as if we have never read from its pages before. Easier said than done. Passages from Scripture are entrenched in our culture and have been infused with certain imagery and emotions, an effect compounded if you grew up in church. But the point is, behind the words of the Bible beats the heart of God, and we should strive to encounter His message and meaning in a fresh way every time we open our Bibles.

Maybe a good first step is to slow down. Emphasize small chunks of Scripture rather than long passages. Go over the words more than once, even out loud if you'd like. And let their meaning penetrate your heart. The important thing is that if you've not established the regular practice of reading God's Word, get started! As you read, realize that God is speaking directly to you.

We have the prophetic word made more sure, to
which you do well to pay attention as to a lamp shining
in a dark place, until the day dawns and the morning star
arises in your hearts. But know this first of all, that no prophecy
of Scripture becomes a matter of someone's own interpretation,
for no prophecy was ever made by an act of human will,
but men moved by the Holy Spirit spoke from God.

2 PETER 1:19-21 NASB

THE CREEPING
WILDERNESS

No great company sets a goal to slide into mediocrity. No in-love newlyweds plan to divorce down the road. No fit, muscular athlete figures out how to put on a hundred pounds and get totally out of shape in the next few years. No neighborhood holds a meeting to outline steps toward a run-down community. No committed, vibrant Christian dreams of a day when he or she will walk far from God, living a life of joyless compromise.

The common denominator in all the above too-often-true scenarios is neglect. The wilderness does not swallow up a great city in a day, it creeps closer and closer—through neglect.

Prayer. A community of believers. God's Word. These are neglected at great risk to our souls!

Whoever heeds discipline shows the way to life.
PROVERBS 10:17

MAKE A PLAN

Every Bible reader has a favorite verse or book, one he or she returns to often for comfort and wisdom. But as wonderful as those familiar favorites can be, there are countless other precious gems in Scripture waiting to be discovered. The only way to find them is to read what we've never read before. That's why a Bible reading plan can be such a valuable tool for spiritual growth.

Your Bible may have a reading plan near the front that will direct you to finish the whole Bible in one year. If not, there are plenty of other ways to read a wider range of Scripture than you ever have before. Search online for reading plans. Some sites offer plans you can even check off as you go along. Consider Bible software or even a program for your smartphone that can provide you with a passage of Scripture every day. Select an unfamiliar book of the Bible each month and read through it with a friend. Whatever method or plan you use, ask God to help you grow in love for His Word.

All his laws are before me;
I have not turned away from his decrees.

PSALM 18:22

SOAKING IN THE WORD

One of the benefits of God's Word is a cleansing and renewing of our minds. How does that happen? Our minds and hearts are pulled away from problems, disappointments, challenges, temptations, failures, resentments, and other negative thoughts and emotions and are redirected to God's thoughts, God's feelings, God's promises, God's principles. But this isn't just an exercise in self-help and guided thoughts. We are told in Hebrews that the Word of God is "living and active" (4:12 NASB). God's words aren't just ink on a page or bytes on an electronic device. Because they have been spoken by God Himself, they have a special way of touching us and renewing us in our inner core.

Are you worried, angry, tempted, distracted, resentful? Why not bathe in God's Word right now? It's good to read through the full range of writings from the Bible, but for this activity, pick a short passage from the Psalms or New Testament. Read it slowly a couple of times. Ask God to speak to you while you read each time. Memorize a key phrase or two. Repeat those phrases throughout your day. Truly bask and soak in the heart of God as you savor His words to you.

I reach out for your commands, which I love,
that I may meditate on your decrees.

PSALM 119:48

FALSE INTERPRETATION

When Martin Luther made the proclamation of "sola scriptura" as the only authority for the Christian's life, part of the phrase has been commonly ignored. He actually said, "Scripture rightly divided," which simply means, "interpreted correctly."

One of the most important reasons to read God's Word and know it ourselves is that it protects us from false prophets. In every age of the church there have been men and women who use the Bible for their own purposes, not to build God's kingdom.

We don't need to live in a posture of skepticism and overanalyze every word from a Bible teacher's lips. But we do need to know God's Word well enough to know when someone has an agenda that is not God's.

> *There were also false prophets among the people, just as there will be false teachers among you. They will secretly introduce destructive heresies, even denying the sovereign Lord who bought them—bringing swift destruction on themselves.*
>
> 2 Peter 2:1

FINDING TRUTH

One of the prevailing temptations of our pluralistic, highly educated culture is to see truth as relative. Right and wrong, the attributes of God, the need and nature of salvation, and essential beliefs and practices are not considered absolute, but merely suggestive.

Throughout Scripture, we are told that some issues are a matter of personal conscience, so there is plenty of room for debate and personal conviction.

But that doesn't mean all matters—or even most matters—of faith have an element of personal decision. For example, Paul declares that if there is no resurrection of Christ, there is no salvation or promise of heaven available. (See 1 Corinthians 15:12-19.) How do we know what is absolute and what involves choice? There is only one sure source of revelation: God's Word. Listen to good preachers and teachers, but never let them take the place of getting to know God's Word for yourself.

The word of God is alive and active.
Sharper than any double-edged sword, it penetrates
even to dividing soul and spirit, joints and marrow;
it judges the thoughts and attitudes of the heart.

Hebrews 4:12

THE BATTLE SUIT

The Bible is referred to as a sword because we use the strength of the Word of God in spiritual battles. The Bible is effective because truth cuts into the falsehood of sin. It causes the sinner to return to God. It wards off the attacks of Satan. The Word fights on.

As we learn the truths of God's Word, we then have possession of the battle gear necessary to fight the enemy of our souls. We have what will cause him to flee: the sword of God's truth. Jesus said, "If you hold to my teaching, you are really my disciples. Then you will know the truth, and the truth will set you free" (John 8:31-32).

God has given us the power on earth we need to live for Him, but we must be willing to call upon Him and ask Him for help. That begins with a commitment to His Word. God will deliver His children as His Word has promised.

Take the helmet of salvation and the
sword of the Spirit, which is the word of God.

Ephesians 6:17

BLESSED IS THE
ONE WHO READS

Peter and John were with Jesus shortly before His return to His Father's right side. In a poignant conversation, Jesus foretold Peter's violent death as a martyr and John's long life. (See John 21:18-24.) All the other apostles died at the hands of those who persecuted the Christian faith, but John died of old age as an exile on the island of Patmos. It was there that he received a vision that came directly from God, which is known as the Book of Revelation, the final entry in the New Testament.

This is not just a book of prophecy, but a hard look at how believers—now and then—live in the present. In John's preface, he provides a word of wisdom all of us of faith are wise to heed: "Blessed is the one who reads aloud the words of this prophecy, and blessed are those who hear it and take to heart what is written in it, because the time is near" (1:3). We are reminded that the "Day" is near, that true strength in times of judgment and difficulty is found in a faithful reading of God's Word.

Blessed is the one who reads aloud the words of this prophecy,
and blessed are those who hear it and take to heart
what is written in it, because the time is near.

REVELATION 1:3

OVERCOMING DISTORTION

Read through the book of Acts in a single setting and you will discover a major transition at chapter 11. In the first ten chapters, the leading man, the hero of the faith, is Peter. But in chapter 11, it is Paul who becomes the leading figure. This makes sense on the basis of 1:8, where we find the outline of the book—and the marching orders for the early believers—to share the gospel in Jerusalem, Samaria, and the ends of the earth. Paul, the great missionary, is the one who took Jesus to the Roman Empire—the ends of the earth.

Peter was obviously acquainted with Paul's writings (his thirteen letters) and admits they can be tough to understand. But his warning about our responsibility in handling God's Word is crystal clear. We are to be careful in how we interpret and teach the words of the Bible. Those who are careless with God's Word—or worse, those who deliberately distort it—will be held accountable.

Be bold in sharing God's Word with others, but always with respect and reverence.

He writes the same way in all his letters, speaking in them of these matters. His letters contain some things that are hard to understand, which ignorant and unstable people distort, as they do the other Scriptures, to their own destruction.

2 PETER 3:16

CLOTHED IN HUMILITY

In the classic children's story of the emperor's new clothes, the emperor was visited by two swindlers who promised that if he provided them with gold thread, they would produce for him the finest clothes in the world. But not just any clothes, magical clothes—only those who were smart and fit for their position could see the clothes they made, they promised. That really appealed to his pride.

You know the rest of the story. The emperor paraded through the streets naked, unwilling to admit that he couldn't see the clothes he was wearing (or not wearing). A simple child pointed out that he was wearing nothing, and the emperor was humiliated in front of the whole town. And so were those who pretended to see his clothes.

You will never accidentally leave the house in the buff believing you're wearing fine clothes, and hopefully you will never fall victim to a shady swindler. But all of us are vulnerable to the sin of pride. Even foolish pride. It makes smart people do dumb things.

Wisdom comes from a proper respect for God and a humble walk before Him.

He guides the humble in what is right and teaches them his way.
All the ways of the LORD are loving and faithful toward
those who keep the demands of his covenant.

PSALM 25:9-10

STAY CONNECTED

Movement, growth, work, force, life itself—all require energy. The power source for the Christian life is connection to Jesus Christ. Jesus paints a picture of a vineyard. It may spread over acres, but every living branch that bears fruit is connected to the vine.

Often, when we don't feel like we are effective in our service— as a spouse, a parent, a minister, a volunteer—we focus on techniques. We think of better methods and programs for making a difference. Maybe we need to first take a step backwards and ask ourselves a few simple questions: How connected am I to Jesus Christ? Am I close to Him? Does He have my faith and love? It's amazing how everything else falls into place when that question is answered positively.

Are you bearing fruit? Are you connected to the vine?

I am the vine; you are the branches. If you remain in me and I in you, you will bear much fruit; apart from me you can do nothing.

JOHN 15:5

GOD'S PLANS

As a young man, William Carey worked as a shoemaker living in London. He was fascinated by explorers and missionaries, anyone who traveled to foreign lands. And his interest in other cultures soon became a deeply felt compassion for the lost and needy of the whole world. Some reported that on the walls of his shop, he hung hand-drawn maps of other countries, annotated with information he found about the climate, diet, and religions of various areas of the world. He built a globe from scraps of leather left over from the shoes he made, and he regularly prayed over it for the people of each country that he thought had never heard the gospel message. And later in life, he became a missionary to India and served many with the message and love of Christ.

Whether or not you serve on an overseas mission field, God has given all of us a calling. How do you find out what yours is? You can probably find it in your areas of interest. You might not think your passions in life are very useful, but in God's hands, they can be used to help and serve others.

"I know the plans I have for you," declares the LORD,
"plans to prosper you and not to harm you,
plans to give you hope and a future."

JEREMIAH 29:11

LED BY THE SPIRIT

Don't know where God wants you to serve? Just ask Him to show you, and then keep your eyes open to the opportunities all around you. Many will come as a complete surprise:

- On a rescheduled flight, you sit next to someone dealing with spiritual issues.

- A wrong turn takes you by an outreach center you had never heard of.

- A waitress opens up and shares some difficulties she is experiencing.

- A conflict with a neighbor becomes the open door for a new relationship.

Paul had plans to minister in Bithynia. God had plans for him to minister in Macedonia—and introduce the good news to a whole new continent (see Acts 16:6-10). He was led by the Spirit. And the same Spirit of God will lead you too.

Paul and his companions traveled throughout the region of Phrygia and Galatia, having been kept by the Holy Spirit from preaching the word in the province of Asia.

ACTS 16:6

BEAR ONE
ANOTHER'S BURDENS

We are not responsible to carry certain burdens of others. In Galatians 6:5, Paul wrote that "each one should carry their own load." Another translation for the word "load" in that verse would be a "backpack." All of us are able to carry a certain amount of weight in life. In fact, doing things for others that they should do for themselves can lead to a cycle of codependence that is unhealthy for the one not pulling his own weight—and for the one carrying multiple backpacks.

But there are some burdens that are excessive. They are too heavy for one person to lift alone. Physical disabilities, emotional trauma, and other burdens can crush one's spirit through sheer magnitude. In cases like this, Paul said we can fulfill the law of Christ by helping someone carry the load. Is there someone in your life who needs you to share the love of Christ with him or her? Are you willing to help someone carry that weight?

Carry each other's burdens, and in this way
you will fulfill the law of Christ.

GALATIANS 6:2

GOD'S GIFT OF REST

According to Genesis 2:2, even God rested after creating the universe. And unlike God, we get tired. When our bodies and brains are tired, they don't function like they were created to and need renewal. But just as much as physical rest, we need to recharge our spirits as well. We need to take a moment at the end of the day to simply breathe slowly and say a short prayer in order to take care of our souls.

Few men lived as intense a life as King David. Kingdom builder and warrior, he faced strife and danger—some of it self-induced—his entire adult life. An emotional man who was subject to the same laws of fatigue and exhaustion as the rest of us, is it any wonder he described the blessed man as one who meditates on God in the morning and at night (Psalm 1:2)?

Sometimes we run the risk of burning ourselves out even in serving God. Don't wait until the point of exhaustion to take time to slow down, thank God, and ask Him for His help and grace.

By the seventh day God had finished the work he had been doing;
so on the seventh day he rested from all his work.

GENESIS 2:2

THE LION'S DEN

When you follow God's call on your life, you might find yourself in some unfamiliar places. A seedy part of town. On stage, speaking in front of a large group. A completely different country. You might get a little scared. And that's okay. What's important to remember is that God is always with you.

Remember Daniel in the lion's den? He was kept overnight in a sealed pit with hungry lions, but when morning came, he shouted from the bottom, "My God sent his angel, and he shut the mouths of the lions. They have not hurt me, because I was found innocent in his sight" (Daniel 6:22). You probably won't be thrown into a literal pit of lions, but you might find yourself under pressure as you serve God. Whatever happens—whether God delivers you miraculously or simply gives you strength to cope—know that He is near you, pleased with you, helping you, turning a lion's den into a sanctuary of praise.

God has said, "Never will I leave you;
never will I forsake you."

HEBREWS 13:5

SPIRITUAL GIFTS

Albert Schweitzer, winner of the Nobel Peace Prize in 1952, was a biblical scholar (often a controversial one), a medical doctor and missionary, and a celebrated musician. Few people achieve his success in even one arena, let alone three. In the eyes of God, however, it would seem that Schweitzer was not greater than anyone else who uses their talents to their utmost in the service of others, whether those talents are musical gifts, physical strength, or a compassionate heart.

Jesus's parable of the talents gives us some perspective. The master gave his servants a number of talents, "each according to his ability" (Matthew 25:15). The ones who multiplied their talents were rewarded, but the servant who simply buried his talent faced punishment. It's a sobering thought: We will be judged on how well we use our abilities. Even if we have fewer than someone else, we must always put what we have to use.

The gifts and abilities God gives us are to be used for God's kingdom, in service to Him and others. Each time we serve in this way, we increase the potential of our gift.

His master replied, "Well done, good and faithful servant!
You have been faithful with a few things; I will put you in charge
of many things. Come and share your master's happiness!"

MATTHEW 25:23

WHEN SERVICE HURTS

In the New Testament, Paul stands as an icon of sacrificial service. He endured beatings and floggings (2 Corinthians 11:25), he wept over wayward and hurtful congregations (2 Corinthians 2:4), and he frequently went without (Philippians 4:12). Yet he affirmed, "I can do everything through Christ, who gives me strength" (Philippians 4:13 NLT).

God does not give all of us the same gifts, and He does not call us all to the same vocation. But all of us are called to humility. Paul told the Philippian church, "Have the same mindset as Christ Jesus: Who, being in very nature God, did not consider equality with God something to be used to his own advantage; rather, he made himself nothing" (Philippians 2:5-7). It can be painful to serve God and others to the point of sacrifice. But as Paul discovered, God supplies our every need along the way.

Even if I am being poured out like a drink offering
on the sacrifice and service coming from your faith,
I am glad and rejoice with all of you.

PHILIPPIANS 2:17

GOD AT WORK

A father and his young son returned home after a trip to the grocery store. The son loved being with his dad and wanted to help him finish the chore. In fact, he wanted to carry the largest bag—which was much too heavy for him—inside. The father had a simple solution. He put the bag in his son's arms and then picked him up and carried both inside.

What a lovely picture of how our heavenly Father works within us. He loves our willingness to take on any assignment. But He knows what we can and cannot do in our strength. When the load is too heavy, the assignment too big, He honors our willing spirit by lifting us up and allowing us to do His work. He empowers us to accomplish more than we can in our own strength.

Do all you can—but realize it is God's power working through you that makes the difference.

It is God who works in you to will and to act
in order to fulfill his good purpose.

PHILIPPIANS 2:13

GIFTS TO GIVE

Go ahead and try. You can't do it. It's impossible to give and not get something in return. Oh, there will be times you extend love and not have it reciprocated. You might give sacrificially from limited funds and still be short on cash. It is possible to help others get their lives in order only to be left completely alone in a moment of need. None of those things are likely, but they are possible.

But you still can't come up empty-handed. It's not possible. Because God, your heavenly Father, sees your gifts of love and is pleased. Even if no one else thanks you, know that He will reward your kindness.

You are likely to receive a return on your investment of service in this lifetime. But even if you don't, you can rest assured that the very best rewards are eternal.

The generous will themselves be blessed.

PROVERBS 22:9

PAY IT FORWARD

The concept of "pay it forward" is built on the idea that people have done good things for you that you can't repay, so you show your gratitude by doing something good for someone who can't repay you. You simply pay it forward.

The ultimate expression of paying it forward is what Jesus Christ did for each of us. Even when we were sinners, even when we were enemies with God, He died for us so we could experience eternal life.

How do we pay that gift forward? Simple. We can never repay Him for His sacrificial love toward us, so we share His love with others who need the gift of life. When was the last time you paid it forward?

> *Let your light shine before others, that they may see*
> *your good deeds and glorify your Father in heaven.*
>
> MATTHEW 5:16

YOU HAVE A PURPOSE

I'm not sure I have a purpose in life. I don't know what I am supposed to do to make the world better.

You might be right. You might not personally have a purpose in life. But there's good news. *God* has a purpose for you. When He created you, He fashioned you in such a way that you could accomplish things that build His kingdom. But that's not all. There's more good news. Not only did He create you with the ability to accomplish great things, He also prepared specific tasks that would utilize your gifts.

Maybe it's a person only you can reach. Maybe it's a ministry you are supposed to start. Maybe it's a gift of encouragement you are to lavish on hundreds and thousands of people. Look in your heart. Look around you. Ask God to open your eyes. And get busy!

We are God's handiwork, created in Christ Jesus to do
good works, which God prepared in advance for us to do.

Ephesians 2:10

CHARITY

Is it possible to do good things for the wrong reasons? Absolutely. Does that mean these good deeds are worthless and achieve no good ends? Not necessarily. Your good deeds, done for the wrong reasons, may very well bless others tremendously. However, the benefit to you and your soul is negated.

Faith without actions is a dead faith, but conversely, actions without love are rarely as effective in making a lasting difference in the world—and are spiritually dead for the one who is doing them.

We experience peace and joy when there is agreement between our internal beliefs and our external actions. Is it time for you to ask God to kindle within you a love for others? Is it time to express your love and faith in tangible acts?

> *Suppose a brother or sister is without clothes and daily*
> *food. If one of you says to them, "Go in peace; keep*
> *warm and well fed," but does nothing about their*
> *physical needs, what good is it? In the same way, faith*
> *by itself, if it is not accompanied by action, is dead.*
>
> JAMES 2:15-17

ON THE FRONT LINES

The life of first responders—EMTs, firefighters, police officers, and others—is undeniably stressful and challenging when emergencies strike. They go through extensive and continual training to be ready for such moments. And they must always be ready for whatever comes their way, whether it's the grisly scene of an accident or the duty of informing a stranger that their loved one won't be coming home. Some days, nothing big happens. Other days, something huge happens.

God calls us to be ever vigilant, always ready to explain our hope in God to someone who doesn't believe in Him, always alert to spiritual attacks, quick with love and kindness to those in need. We never know when someone around us might need God to work through us.

Are you ready to spring into action?

Be ready to do whatever is good.

Titus 3:1

GO WITH JOY

Bad habits are easier to form than good habits. It's easier to wallow in a bad attitude than to change the way we look at life in a positive way. Those principles are true of both groups and individuals.

What is the attitude of the various groups you belong to? Your neighborhood friends? Your work department? Your family? Your church? Is there a spirit of negativity and complaining—or a spirit of joy? Most importantly, what attitude do you bring to the table?

Are you positive or negative? Do you go forth into the world with a contagious joy—where even mountains and hills begin to shout—or do you succumb to a prevailing negativity? The choice is yours!

You will go out in joy and be led forth in peace;
the mountains and hills will burst into song before you,
and all the trees of the field will clap their hands.

Isaiah 55:12

REJOICE IN THE SUCCESS OF OTHERS

We live in a competitive world where it is difficult for many people to find joy in the success of others. How do you feel when a friend gets a promotion? When someone else in the company wins the award? When a classmate gets the top score on a test? When a sibling gets an incredible return on an investment? Do you feel instant joy or pangs of resentment and jealousy?

We are often much better at comforting someone in their times of sorrow than sincerely celebrating their moments of triumph.

The answer is simple but difficult: We must first realize our own success is measured in the eyes of God—not in comparison with others. When that sinks into our hearts and minds, it is so much easier to rejoice in the success of others. Sincerely.

Rejoice with those who rejoice;
mourn with those who mourn.

ROMANS 12:15

JOY FOR ETERNITY

It's been said that those who let their minds dwell on heaven are of no earthly good. But is it possible that the opposite is true? The history of the Christian church is filled with accounts that those who thought most of heaven did the most good here on earth.

The realization that this present life is not all there is gives one a perspective that every moment here on earth counts. It challenges us to walk closely with God so we don't miss an eternity in heaven with Him—and to put our hands to the task of bringing friends, family members, and loved ones along with us.

Do you live your life today with the understanding that the much greater portion of your existence will be spent after your death? Are you making your life count in eternity? And are you inviting others to enjoy the presence of God for eternity with you?

Then I saw "a new heaven and a new earth,"
for the first heaven and the first earth had passed away,
and there was no longer any sea.

REVELATION 21:1

THE CHOICE TO BE HAPPY

Do we have a choice when it comes to joy?

The apostle James says, "Consider it pure joy, my brothers and sisters, whenever you face trials of many kinds" (James 1:2). Paul says, "Rejoice in the Lord always. I will say it again: Rejoice!" (Philippians 4:4). Jesus said to His disciples, "Do not let your hearts be troubled and do not be afraid" (John 14:27).

Is joy a choice? The biblical answer is clearly yes. But throughout Scripture there is a strong recognition that it is not always an easy choice. Life can be tough. We get hurt. There are disappointments. Sometimes circumstances seem to conspire against us. And yet as an act of worship, as a matter of prayer, as a declaration of faith, as an act of love for Jesus, we can choose joy. Just the fact that God has given us a choice to experience joy is a reason to rejoice.

> *We proclaim to you what we have seen and heard,*
> *so that you also may have fellowship with us. And our*
> *fellowship is with the Father and with his Son, Jesus*
> *Christ. We write this to make our joy complete.*
>
> 1 JOHN 1:3-4

HARVEST TIME

Every year, farmers go into a flurry of activity when harvest time arrives. The memory of the long hours of hard labor necessary to guarantee a good crop seems to fade in the distance. They feel pride at seeing the finished results of all their work—grain, vegetables, and livestock that will feed many people.

We all experience harvest times in our lives, whether we own a farm or can't keep a houseplant alive. We must work hard toward our goals, whether they're professional, personal, or spiritual. But if we're persistent and diligent, we'll experience a harvest. We'll reap rewards from our labors. And that's a very special kind of joy, the thrill of hard work paying off.

He makes grass grow for the cattle, and plants for
people to cultivate—bringing forth food from the earth:
wine that gladdens human hearts, oil to make their
faces shine, and bread that sustains their hearts.

PSALM 104:14-15

TOO EASILY PLEASED

Could it be that so many in our modern culture are unhappy because they have mistaken fleeting pleasures for a deep abiding joy, and in so doing, have treasured unworthy ends? C.S. Lewis probed this thought when he said: "Indeed, if we consider the unblushing promises of reward and the staggering nature of the rewards promised in the Gospels, it would seem that our Lord finds our desires not too strong, but too weak. We are half-hearted creatures, fooling around with drink and sex and ambition when infinite joy is offered us, like an ignorant child who wants to go on making mud pies in the slum because he cannot imagine what is meant by the offer of a holiday at the sea. We are far too easily pleased."

All of us need a spiritual checkup from time to time to make sure our hearts and our desires are in line with God's will for our lives. Where do you find your pleasure? What do you consider your treasure? Have you given your heart to something of infinite worth?

Where your treasure is, there your heart will be also.

MATTHEW 6:21

THANK GOD
FOR HAPPINESS

Into every life a little rain must fall. Sometimes things go wrong. But sometimes things go right. And when they do, James says, we should praise God.

What's going right in your life today—what is making you happy? Is there a relationship in your life that's thriving? Do you have the simple blessings of a job and reliable transportation to work? Have you found an activity or service opportunity that brings you joy? You might have to do a little looking around and count your blessings—sometimes those little reasons for joy and gratitude get overlooked. But when you find something to be happy about, be happy.

When we find ourselves in trouble, we need to turn to God for help and strength. But when things are going well, we—again—need to turn to God. He deserves our thanksgiving for the good things He gives us.

Is anyone among you in trouble? Let them pray.
Is anyone happy? Let them sing songs of praise.

JAMES 5:13

KEEP IN STEP

What goes into living the Christian life? Many traditions of the faith have answered that question with certain emphases and nuances, but three common traits have always been part of the Christian walk: faith, trust, and obedience.

Faith is a belief in the reality of God, the goodness and love of God, and the relationship God desires to have with us. "Now faith is the assurance of what we hope for and the certainty of what we do not see" (Hebrews 11:1 BSB). Trust is an ongoing expression of faith. It is placing our confidence in God and depending on Him every step of the way. It is our basis for assurance that God is with us in all circumstances of life. "Though he slay me, yet will I hope in him" (Job 13:15).

Obedience is when we acknowledge that Jesus is not only our Savior—but our Lord. It is the full expression of faith, where we trust God so much we submit to His commands, His ways, His will. "But if we walk in the light, as he is in the light, we have fellowship with one another, and the blood of Jesus, his Son, purifies us from all sin" (1 John 1:7).

Since we live by the Spirit,
let us keep in step with the Spirit.

GALATIANS 5:25

THE BENEFITS
OF OBEDIENCE

We all know there are negative consequences to disobeying God, but do we ever stop to consider all the blessings and rewards that come to us through obedience? Have we made obedience a drudgery that steals the fun from life, rather than affirming how much sweeter and better it makes life? There are more rewards and blessings from obedience than can be listed on a single page, but consider the following as you look up the corresponding Bible verses.

- Obedience gives us a clean conscience (Psalm 19:13).
- Obedience keeps us from danger (Psalm 91:10).
- Obedience brings material blessings (Deuteronomy 11:13-15).
- Obedience prolongs life (Deuteronomy 11:9).
- Obedience is a blessing to our family (Psalm 112:1-3).
- Obedience brings joy (Psalm 119:33-35).
- Obedience increases our faith (James 2:17).

I reach out for your commands, which I love,
that I may meditate on your decrees.

PSALM 119:48

USE YOUR TALENTS

There is a familiar story of three men who were given varying talents by their master. (See Matthew 25:14-30.) The man with the most talents did the most. *Not surprising.* The man with the second most talents came in second place. *Not unexpected.* The third man did absolutely nothing. *Of course. He didn't have enough to make a difference.* When the master saw that he had buried what was given to him, he took it away.

Is that fair? What if he had lost the meager amount on a bad investment? Wouldn't he have been in bigger trouble? Jesus's story doesn't seem to indicate that. He says nothing about being judged on the basis of failing. Judgment is based on doing nothing, burying the talents God has given us.

What resources has God given you to work with in life? Has He given you a lot or a little or something in between? Your answer isn't important. All that matters is what you're going to do with what you've got. What investment do you need to make in your world?

Use whatever gift you have received to serve others,
as faithful stewards of God's grace in its various forms.

1 PETER 4:10

TWO BROTHERS

The Bible is filled with famous brothers. Cain and Abel. Jacob and Esau. Peter and Andrew. The prodigal and his older brother. But there are two unnamed brothers that Jesus introduced in a parable. (See Matthew 21:28-31.) Their father gave each an assignment. The first brother moaned and complained and said, "No way." The second brother had a great attitude and immediately told his father, "No problem, I'm on it."

At the end of the day, the second brother with a great attitude had done a great job and the first brother with a bad attitude was still pouting and sullen. Right?

Wrong! The second brother got distracted and never got after it. The first brother thought better of his refusal and got the job done. Jesus asked, "Which one obeyed?" Easy answer. The one who got it done.

A good attitude is better than a bad attitude, but actions still speak louder than words. Have a bad attitude over a task God has placed before you? Just get busy and it'll disappear before you know it.

Whoever does the will of my Father in heaven
is my brother and sister and mother.

Matthew 12:50

BE FRUITFUL

One of Paul's faithful coworkers in his missionary travels throughout the Roman Empire was Titus. Paul left Titus on the island of Crete to encourage and establish order in the churches there (Titus 1:5). He instructed Titus by repeating his common theme that salvation is not a matter of works but God's kindness: "When the kindness and love of God our Savior appeared, he saved us, not because of righteous things we had done, but because of his mercy" (Titus 3:4-5).

But in verse 14 he appealed to an image from farming. Fruitfulness does not happen unless seeds of good works and acts of love are planted: "Our people must learn to devote themselves to doing what is good, in order to provide for urgent needs and not live unproductive lives" (Titus 3:14).

Fall is coming and your fruitfulness will be in measure with the seeds of love and obedience you've planted. What seeds will you plant today?

Our people must learn to devote themselves to doing what is good, in order to provide for urgent needs and not live unproductive lives.

Titus 3:14

THE WRONG KIND OF PRIDE

The sin of pride can be hard to define. Arrogance can be part of it, yes. But it's possible to have both pride and poor self-image at work in one's life at the same time. God doesn't want us to lack self-respect, either. Maybe it's best simply to be ever aware that all of us are vulnerable to vain pride and that it can find us anytime, anywhere.

Pride says, "I can do what I want," "I'm better than others," and "I'm looking out for number one." Above all, pride says, "I don't need God or anyone—I can make it on my own." But of course, we do need God. And when we resist surrendering to Him, depending on Him, we experience damage to our souls.

Fortunately, we can resist our pride by simply praying and asking God to heal us from a prideful attitude and help us think rightly about ourselves, God, and others. When that happens, we can rest content in God's will and at peace with ourselves and those around us.

When pride comes, then comes disgrace,
but with humility comes wisdom.

PROVERBS 11:2

TAKE THE RIGHT PATH

It's not that hard to take a wrong turn in life. Doing the wrong thing, if we're honest, has an allure. It's called temptation. When we look around, it's common to spot someone who has gone astray—wayward sons, daughters, friends, and acquaintances fill prisons and homeless shelters, church pews, and cubicles alike.

The good news is that when we repent, God can turn us around and help us find our way again. The better news is that He offers plenty of advice for how to live well in the world so that we can avoid going off the rails in the first place. The book of Proverbs alone is a treasure trove of principles for living: work hard, watch the time, don't live just for pleasure, make following God your primary concern. These aren't burdensome rules—they're simply guidelines for living the game of life well and effectively.

Open your Bible and let God lead you today. He'll show you the right path to take.

> *We all, like sheep, have gone astray,*
> *each of us has turned to our own way;*
> *and the LORD has laid on him the iniquity of us all.*
>
> ISAIAH 53:6

AN EMERGENCY CALLED COMPLACENCY

Complacency is a blight that saps energy, dulls attitudes, and causes a drain on the brain. The first symptom is satisfaction with things as they are. The second is rejection of things as they might be. "Good enough" becomes today's watchword and tomorrow's standard. Complacency makes people fear the unknown, mistrust the untried, and abhor the new. Like water, complacent people follow the easiest course—downhill. They draw false strength from looking back.

But God has given us certain responsibilities that require attention and action on our part. Our lives need upkeep, and we must be careful not to neglect these matters that require a non-complacent vigilance of attitude. Priority one is making sure we are following God. He does not force us to choose Him. But when we do, we experience His blessing.

Let us throw off everything that hinders
and the sin that so easily entangles.

Hebrews 12:1

LOSING TO GAIN

As he gained speed going down a hill, the young boy racing along on his bike saw a sharp turn just ahead. But the speed was exhilarating, so he paused a second—and then another and another—reluctant to apply the brakes. So he hit the curve at full speed. When he hit a bump, he lost control and found himself flying off the bike. Both he and the bicycle were a bit mangled, but survived. But he learned the simple truth that sometimes we must give up something we enjoy in order to get something better—or simply to survive. That is true in the physical world, but even more so in the spiritual realm.

Jesus said, "Whoever wants to save their life will lose it, but whoever loses their life for me and for the gospel will save it" (Mark 8:35). Giving something up in obedience to God might sting a little. But in the end, it's the only course for keeping our bike on the road and living our best possible life.

Anyone who loves their life will lose it,
while anyone who hates their life in this world
will keep it for eternal life.

JOHN 12:25

THE RIPPLES OF DISOBEDIENCE

When we are disobedient to God's will and ways, we create a negative impact not only for ourselves, but often for those around us. Ever since the sin of Adam and Eve in the Garden of Eden, the consequences of disobedience have been staggering. Cain's disobedience led to Abel's murder. David's infidelity led to the death of a trusted comrade—and ultimately the splitting of a kingdom. Judas's betrayal abetted Jesus's arrest.

There's a vital life-and-death lesson in these Bible stories for all of us. Even if some people seem to get away with wrongdoing—maybe even prosper in it—there is a price to pay for disobedience, and even if we swear we'll cover the whole bill ourselves, we can't necessarily protect those around us. If there is a temptation in your life right now that has become even more alluring because you've started to think that acting on it wouldn't hurt anyone else, ask God to check your spirit and provide you with the wisdom and perspective that will help you flee from the very idea of it. Some actions can't be taken back, nor can their consequences be contained or controlled.

The prudent give thought to their steps.

PROVERBS 14:15

LISTEN UP!

The idea of obedience has fallen on hard times in our culture. On one side are those who don't believe obedience in the traditional sense of following a set of moral guidelines is even possible. Another unhealthy view is that obedience is only for those who are not strong or smart enough to order their own lives.

Is there a better, healthier way of looking at obedience? One place to start is with the background of the English word. It is derived from the Latin "obaudire," which means "to listen well." At the heart of obedience in the Bible is relationship. Obedience is based on the deepest level of communication where the other person is heard and understood. For Christians, this means that obedience cannot be reduced to a simple list of dos and don'ts, but is tantamount to an act of worship. We look so closely at God and listen so closely for His voice that we act in ways that show we are engaged in conversation and communion with God.

Obedience. Listening intently. Understanding the heart of another. When looked at that way, how obedient are you in hearing God's voice?

Give me understanding, so that I may
keep your law and obey it with all my heart.

PSALM 119:34

BIG FAITH

God had promised to lead Abraham to a place called Canaan, a "land of promise." Even when things looked hopeless—enemies everywhere, a difficult nephew, his and his wife's inability to have children—Abraham obeyed. And ultimately, despite the obstacles to overcome, he saw God's promise in his life fulfilled.

You may feel like God is calling you into what looks like a forsaken desert. You may not be sure how God's promises will be fulfilled. But like Abraham, you can safely obey, because even though you might not know where you're going, you do know who is leading you. And you know that He has never failed yet.

By faith Abraham, when called to go to a place he would later receive as his inheritance, obeyed and went, even though he did not know where he was going.

HEBREWS 11:8

THE GIFT OF GIVING

One of the true tests of our character is what we do with our money. Of course, God calls us to give a portion of our income to Him through ministry (Numbers 18:28) and also to give special sacrificial offerings to meet special needs as we feel directed in our hearts (Numbers 15:3). Paul does say that some people have a special gift of giving (Romans 12:8), but he also points out that God loves a cheerful giver (2 Corinthians 9:7).

When we are generous with our money above and beyond expectations, we experience a number of benefits: We are more aware that all good gifts come from God, we learn to trust and serve Him with a pure heart, and we receive the joy of helping someone in need. Besides all that, there is a strange paradox that the more we give, the more we seem to have.

As you practice giving generously, God will teach you the wonderful truth that whatever we grasp and hoard dries up and suffocates, but whatever we give freely and generously takes off and soars.

Each of you should give what you have decided
in your heart to give, not reluctantly or under
compulsion, for God loves a cheerful giver.

2 CORINTHIANS 9:7

ONE MAN'S FAITH

In Exodus 14, we read that God commanded the children of Israel to turn on their journey toward the south, which would cause Pharaoh to think that they had lost their way in confusion and would be easy to overtake. As Pharaoh gathered his army of many men and rushed to catch up with the newly freed slaves, the Israelites grew fearful. But Moses obeyed God and stretched his hand over the sea, and it parted for the Israelites to cross to safety.

It's a familiar story, one with many life applications. It tells us of God's might in our weakness and His provision for His people. It also shows how a generation of people can be affected by one person's obedience to God. How can you help steer your generation into a bright future?

Keep this Book of the Law always on
your lips; meditate on it day and night, so that
you may be careful to do everything written in it.
Then you will be prosperous and successful.

Joshua 1:8

A SPECIAL CALL

Throughout Scripture we have accounts of people who were given special tasks, who received a special call on their lives from God. Abraham was called to leave his home country to become the father of God's people. Samson was called to be a Nazarite—a young man who would never touch fermented wine or have his hair cut—in order to show his commitment to God. James and John were two fishermen whom Jesus called to be His disciples. Paul was blinded and knocked off his horse when Jesus called him to be an ambassador of love. The list goes on and on.

God still calls people today. He asks young people to prepare for a life of dedicated ministry—and some middle-aged and older people to leave a career to serve Him in ministry. There are countless other tasks and calls that God gives that are not universal to all the world or everyone who is a believer, but to a specific person. Maybe even you.

When Isaiah worshipped in the temple and felt God's call on his life, his answer was simple: "Here am I. Send me!" (Isaiah 6:8). What will your answer be?

I heard the voice of the Lord saying,
"Whom shall I send? And who will go for us?"
And I said, "Here am I. Send me!"

Isaiah 6:8

RIGHTEOUS DISOBEDIENCE

The apostle Paul reminds us that if we obey our government's laws, we will save ourselves a lot of trouble in life (Romans 13:1-7). But from a biblical perspective, it also appears there is a time when disobedience to a governing body is the proper Christian response. When religious and civil rulers ordered John and Peter to stop preaching the gospel of Jesus Christ, their response was: "We must obey God rather than human beings!" (Acts 5:29). Even today, all over the world, more Christians are killed for their faith each year than in the first two thousand years combined.

Our freedom to express our faith sometimes seems under assault, but we still enjoy legal protection of worship and—for now, at least—don't have to defy our government to call ourselves Christians. But one thing all of us can do is reflect on our loyalty to God over our loyalty to earthly powers. And all of us can pray for Christian brothers and sisters all over the world whose faith has made them outlaws.

Judge for yourselves whether it is right in God's sight to listen to you rather than God. For we cannot stop speaking about what we have seen and heard.

ACTS 4:19-20 BSB

BY PRAYER

God blesses us every day with things we don't necessarily ask for, things we might take for granted: a place to live, fresh air, the beauty of nature, friends and family. But for some blessings, He chooses to make us part of the process by encouraging us to ask for what we need and want. And the truth is that we experience life and blessings more fully when we look to God for all our wants and needs, either through expressing gratitude or petitioning Him for our needs.

If you're hurting for something today, ask God for it. And if you're not, thank Him for what you have. You'll find your life more richly blessed—even if only from an improved attitude. Best yet, your whole being will be permeated with an awareness of God's presence and goodness.

You do not have because you do not ask God.

JAMES 4:2

WHEN YOU
HAVE NO WORDS

Prayer is so important to our spiritual life, but there's good news when we just don't seem to have the words to pray. First of all, we are told that Jesus Christ is at the right side of God the Father interceding for us. It's always great to have someone put in a good word for us, but think about it: right now, Jesus is doing just that for us. For you. What better reference could we have? But secondly, the Holy Spirit helps us as well. Paul tells us: "He who searches our hearts knows the mind of the Spirit, because the Spirit intercedes for God's people in accordance with the will of God" (Romans 8:27).

Is there a problem in your life you have prayed over for years and can no longer come up with words to pray for it? Are you watching a family member make bad decisions, and you don't know what else to say to God on his or her behalf? Do you feel a heaviness of heart and just can't muster the words to express what you're feeling? Maybe it's okay to just sit quietly and depend on the Holy Spirit to do your praying for you, to tell the Father what you can't quite say yourself.

The Spirit helps us in our weakness. We do not know
what we ought to pray for, but the Spirit himself
intercedes for us through wordless groans.

ROMANS 8:26

THE WISH LIST

Scripture is full of assurances that God will hear and answer our prayers. Of course, there's a danger in taking this wonderful truth and turning God into a personal valet, ready to meet our every whim and fancy. In our praying, we have a responsibility to seek God's will. Our wish is not His command.

Perhaps the best way to avoid turning your prayer time into reciting a wish list is to remember that prayer is a real relationship. It's not magic. God has invited us into a relationship with Him and provided us the means to reach Him, through His Son. When we ask Him for good gifts—something He encourages us to do—we should remember that we're talking to someone who loves us, wants what's best for us, and knows what we really need.

Most importantly, when we go to God in prayer, we are communing with the One who seeks a relationship of love with us.

The prayer of the upright pleases him.

PROVERBS 15:8

LISTEN FOR HIS VOICE

Do you know someone who is a chronic interrupter? Someone who you know isn't really listening to you or others but thinking of what to say next? Has that someone ever been you? How about in your prayer life? Do you ever present your needs and thanksgiving and then just pause to listen?

Does God still speak directly today? Many of us will never know because we don't stop, quiet our hearts, and listen. When was the last time you truly prayed—without speaking a word? Is today that day for you?

> *After the earthquake came a fire,*
> *but the LORD was not in the fire.*
> *And after the fire came a gentle whisper.*

1 KINGS 19:12

UNTIL THE END

While very ill, John Knox, the founder of the Presbyterian Church in Scotland, called to his wife and said, "Read me that Scripture where I first cast my anchor." After he listened to the beautiful prayer of Jesus recorded in John 17, he seemed to forget his weakness. He began to pray, interceding earnestly for his fellow men. He prayed for the ungodly who had thus far rejected the gospel. He pleaded on behalf of people who had been recently converted. And he requested protection for the Lord's servants, many of whom were facing persecution. As Knox prayed, his spirit went home to be with the Lord. The man of whom Queen Mary had said, "I fear his prayers more than I do the armies of my enemies," ministered through prayer until the moment of his death.

There are many needs around us—our neighbors, family, friends, and coworkers could all use a touch from God in some area or another. We have the privilege of bringing those needs to God in prayer. And we are blessed when we do so.

Let us not become weary in doing good,
for at the proper time we will reap
a harvest if we do not give up.

GALATIANS 6:9

A CALL TO PRAYER

In September of 1857, Jeremiah Lanphier, a city minister, began a weekly noon prayer meeting in New York that by October had grown into a daily prayer meeting attended by hundreds of businessmen. By March of the next year, newspapers carried front-page reports that over 6,000 were attending daily prayer meetings in downtown New York and Pittsburgh, and similar meetings were being held in Washington at five different times to accommodate the crowds. By May 1859, 50,000 New Yorkers had reported accepting Christ through these meetings.

It might be hard to envision a similar resurgence of faith in our own time. But the biggest movements often begin with the smallest steps of prayer. What would happen if you began meeting with just a few friends to pray? Why not try it and see?

Every day they continued to meet together in the temple courts. They broke bread in their homes and ate together with glad and sincere hearts, praising God and enjoying the favor of all the people. And the Lord added to their number daily those who were being saved.

ACTS 2:46-47

AN ETERNAL IMPACT

What a wonderful heritage in the faith Timothy had. Paul considered this young man more than a protégé, he looked at Timothy as a son (1 Corinthians 4:17). But Paul knew that Timothy's godly heritage began long before he took him under his wing on his missionary journeys. Timothy had a mother and grandmother who prayed for him from his childhood (2 Timothy 1:5). Did you grow up in that kind of family? Even if you didn't, there is a good chance someone prayed for you and was instrumental in your relationship with God.

Even if you can't answer that question, it raises an even more important question for you to consider right now. For whom are you praying regularly? Who will say your prayers gave them the encouragement they needed in a tough time to draw even closer to God? Whom might you meet in heaven because you would not stop praying for their very soul here on earth?

You have the power to make a difference in the kingdom of God simply by praying for those close to you. Don't miss out on seeing blessings in their lives.

I am reminded of your sincere faith, which first lived in
your grandmother Lois and in your mother Eunice
and, I am persuaded, now lives in you also.

2 TIMOTHY 1:5

CHANGE OF PLANS

It is true to say that God never changes. "Jesus Christ is the same yesterday and today and forever," Hebrews tells us (13:8). But that verse is referring to His nature: He is always good and holy and loving and merciful. It is also true to say that often what changes most when we pray, is us. We ask God to change a situation and instead He changes us. He doesn't always make our burdens smaller—sometimes He makes us stronger.

But sometime our prayers convince God to intervene in a situation in a way He would not have had we not prayed. Because of the Hebrew children's flagrant disobedience, God intended to destroy them (Exodus 32:9). But Moses prayed that God would not do so, and God changed His mind (verses 11-14). Have you ever considered that you can convince God to act in a brand-new way in a situation because He responds to the urgency of your heart and prayers? This in no way makes God less or smaller than He is. But it does show that He responds to the prayers of His children.

He took note of their distress when he heard their cry;
for their sake he remembered his covenant
and out of his great love he relented.

Psalm 106:44-45

CONSISTENTLY AND PERSISTENTLY

Jesus spoke in many parables to teach His followers about living in the kingdom of God. In one parable, He told them about a widow who came before a judge with a grievance. She constantly, continually requested that the judge protect her from her adversary. The judge always refused to grant the widow's request, but she was persistent until finally the judge said, "Even though I don't fear God or care what people think, yet because this widow keeps bothering me, I will see that she gets justice, so that she won't eventually come and attack me!" (Luke 18:4-5).

Salespeople know you have to knock on doors persistently and consistently to close a sale. Teachers know repetition is a necessary ingredient if students are to retain what they learn. Constantly coming to God doesn't pester Him. But it does keep our own focus on Him.

> *Jesus told his disciples a parable to show them*
> *that they should always pray and not give up.*
>
> LUKE 18:1

HEARING GOD'S VOICE

Music. Television. Traffic and other background noises. The ticking of a clock. Is there ever a moment of quiet and silence for the modern soul? How about you? How do you do without sound? Are you distracted when there are no distractions?

Perhaps we never hear God's voice because we always have some other sound turned on. How would you feel if you were trying to say something to someone with earbuds in their ears connected to a tiny music player? How easy is it to have a conversation when the other person keeps texting or picking up other calls?

Jesus Christ Himself pulled away from crowds for some alone time with His Father. How much more important is that for us?

> *Very early in the morning, while it was still dark, Jesus got up,*
> *left the house and went off to a solitary place, where he prayed.*
>
> MARK 1:35

HINDRANCES TO PRAYER

What keeps you from prayer? Is it worry? Demands on your attention? Boredom? An abundance of entertainment?

Nothing is more important to our spiritual lives than prayer. Jesus taught us to seek the kingdom first (Matthew 6:33), and Paul instructed us to pray without ceasing (1 Thessalonians 5:17). If we desire to follow God, we must pray. So how can you beat those distractions and hindrances?

Try a little separation. Physically remove yourself from your phone, the TV, reading material. You might choose a verse of Scripture and concentrate on it for a few moments before starting to pray. The hard truth is that all the tricks in the world won't make prayer a piece of cake. Sometimes the choice to direct our attention to talking to God is simply an act of will. But take heart: God wants us to pray, and He can help us overcome any obstacles.

Devote yourselves to prayer, keeping alert in it
with an attitude of thanksgiving.

COLOSSIANS 4:2 NASB

PERSONAL INTERACTION

An anonymous author recounted the story of a traveler in China who visited a temple on a feast day, joining many pilgrims in gathering around a sacred shrine. He noticed that many of them were pulling out strips of paper, rolling them in mud, and tossing them at the idol. When he asked what they were doing, he was told that the pieces of paper were written prayers. They believed that if the mud-wrapped paper stuck to the idol, it would serve as a promise that the prayer would be answered. If it fell off, it meant the prayer had been rejected.

There's no easy way to know how God will respond to our prayers. But would we really want there to be? We grow through prayer and communing with God through His Word and connections with fellow believers. If we interacted with God through anything but personal means, would that experience be as rich and engaging?

God is listening. And if we pay attention, we will hear Him speak back, even if our prayers aren't immediately answered.

Trust in him at all times, you people;
pour out your hearts to him, for God is our refuge.

PSALM 62:8

TEACH US TO PRAY

One day when Jesus had just finished praying, one of His disciples came to Him with a request. He wanted Jesus to teach them how to pray. At that moment, Jesus gave His disciples the Lord's Prayer, the model for Christian prayer throughout the centuries. He went on to teach them more about prayer, saying, "Ask and it will be given to you; seek and you will find; knock and the door will be opened to you. For everyone who asks receives; the one who seeks finds; and to the one who knocks, the door will be opened" (Luke 11:9-10).

There is no one better than Jesus Christ to teach us how to relate to and interact with God. He offers us teaching about how to pray, and in the Gospels He models for us a diligent and dedicated prayer life. If we ask Him to, He can show us how to pray effectively.

Lord, teach us to pray, just as John taught his disciples.

LUKE 11:1

RIGHT MOTIVES

No other biblical writer is more pragmatic and in your face than James. In his letter, he puts great emphasis on faith in action. Does this mean he was a legalist who didn't believe in salvation as a gift? Was he calling for us to base our relationship with God on our good works? Not at all. He simply believed that the person who has experienced God's grace will evidence it in his or her daily walk.

James extols the power of prayer—"The prayer of a righteous person is powerful and effective" (5:16)—but he also challenges us to check our motives. Is our prayer focused on an easy life or on doing great things for God? Never stop taking your needs before God, but do pause and check your heart from time to time.

When you ask, you do not receive,
because you ask with wrong motives,
that you may spend what you get on your pleasures.

JAMES 4:3

KEEP IT SIMPLE,
KEEP IT SECRET

In the Sermon on the Mount, Jesus advised His listeners not to pray for show, and not to pray with endless repetition. He told us to keep it simple, and to pray in secret, not flaunting our spirituality before other people. Prayer is meant to be communion with God. When we pray for show, our hearts and minds are on what others think, not what God thinks. And when we pray with many words, we get caught up in the action of prayer and forget to direct our thoughts to God.

There are many simple prayers that can be said quietly and quickly, but deeply express our need for God: "Lord, help." "Lord, have mercy." "Your will be done." All it takes to pray meaningfully is to bring our whole hearts to God. And that can be done in very few words.

When you pray, do not be like the hypocrites, for they love to pray standing in the synagogues and on the street corners to be seen by others. Truly I tell you, they have received their reward in full.

Matthew 6:5

REJOICE

Some days find us more eager to rejoice than others. Some days, something big and wonderful happens in our lives, and joyful feelings flow freely. Other days are difficult, and other days are simply ordinary. Nothing to write home about.

But Paul admonished us to rejoice always (1 Thessalonians 5:16). And whether we realize it or not, we have good reason to. We have the promise of God's love and salvation and His grace to pull us through any circumstance. We also have the promise of His Spirit working within us to make us more like Him and more able to live joyful, productive lives.

When we know God and walk closely with Him, every day can be extraordinary. So rejoice throughout the day!

Sing and make music from your heart to the Lord.

EPHESIANS 5:19

REMEMBER TO REMEMBER

The concept of remembering is an important biblical theme. The command not to forget is given more than four hundred times. We are to remember:

- The wonders of God's creation and works of His hands (Deuteronomy 4:32).
- That the world belongs to God (Psalm 50:10).
- The deliverance of His people from captivity (Deuteronomy 5:15).
- The sacrificial gift of Jesus Christ on the cross (1 Corinthians 11:25).

Remembering is not just about looking at the past. It is about facing the future with confidence. Remembering keeps us from falling into the sin of ingratitude—we remember all that God has done for us and don't take pride in our own abilities and accomplishments. Remembering also gives us encouragement for tough times—we remember that times have been tough before and God helped us through them and know in our hearts He will do so again.

Today have you remembered to remember?

I will remember the deeds of the LORD;
yes, I will remember your miracles of long ago.

PSALM 77:11

THANKFULNESS IN TOUGH TIMES

Habakkuk 3 describes an economic nightmare: the vines were not bearing fruit, the fields were not producing food, livestock was not thriving. When the right (or wrong) conditions conspire, we find ourselves scrambling to get by, staving off desperation, and dreading the future.

Yet even in the midst of crisis, Habakkuk exulted in God. Why? Because God gives strength to keep going. He gives us hinds' feet on high places—He enables us to trod rough terrain as nimbly as a deer.

Unhappy with today and fearful about tomorrow? Stop for a minute, take a deep breath, and consciously express praise and thanks to God. He is at work even if you can't see it. And with eyes of gratitude, you'll probably begin to see more blessings than you did before.

Though there are no sheep in the pen and no cattle in the stalls,
yet I will rejoice in the Lord, I will be joyful in God my
Savior. The Sovereign Lord is my strength.

Habakkuk 3:17-19

THE PRODIGAL SON

Remember the story of the prodigal son? Most retellings of the parable focus closely on the wayward son. But there's another son in the parable, the resentful and grumpy older brother. As the party rang in the distance, he sulked that even though he had never asked his father for anything, he now had to watch him lavish gifts on his ungrateful brother.

Have you ever been the older brother? Have you wondered why God chose to bless someone else, someone who didn't appear to deserve it? If so, the father's words to his son might be meaningful for you as well: "You have always been with me, and all that is mine is yours. But we had to celebrate and rejoice, because this brother of yours was dead and has begun to live, and was lost and has been found" (Luke 15:31-32 NASB).

Like the father in the parable, God richly blesses us every day. When He throws a party for someone else, we should celebrate too, knowing what a good God we have.

Let's have a feast and celebrate. For this son of mine
was dead and is alive again; he was lost and is found.

LUKE 15:23-24

GOOD SOIL

A colloquial story is told of a man who found the barn where Satan stores the seeds he sows in the human heart: envy, greed, anger, hatred, lust, and so on. The man noticed that Satan had more seeds of discouragement than any other kind, and he learned those seeds were hardy and fruitful and could be made to grow almost anywhere. But when Satan was questioned, he reluctantly admitted that there was one place in which he could not get them to grow. "Where is that?" asked the man. Satan replied, "In the heart of a thankful man."

When we choose a thankful attitude, our spirits resist the cynicism, discouragement, and pessimism that weigh life down. We're better able to thrive and survive no matter what life throws at us. And our love for God blooms.

Let the message of Christ dwell among you richly as you teach and admonish one another with all wisdom through psalms, hymns, and songs from the Spirit, singing to God with gratitude in your hearts.

COLOSSIANS 3:6

WE GET WHAT WE GIVE

There's a principle in life that seems oxymoronic at first glance: we get what we give. But a second look shows the wisdom of the principle. When we bless others, we are blessed. When we love, we are loved. When we give—even in the midst of our own needs—we greatly receive. It's possible to give beyond our resources and find ourselves burned out and broke. But over time, if we're willing to give, we'll receive a lot more in return.

Gratitude unlocks the doors of generosity. Even if you're in need, gratitude helps you give to others sacrificially, just like the poor widow Jesus praised (Mark 12:41-44). Do your own soul a favor by sharing generously from the abundance of your life. You'll be grateful you did!

*Give, and it will be given to you. A good measure, pressed down,
shaken together and running over, will be poured into your lap.
For with the measure you use, it will be measured to you.*

LUKE 6:38

THE SECRET OF TRUE WEALTH

A man lives in a mansion in a zip code known for wealth, his garage filled with expensive automobiles. And yet he lives in poverty, for he is miserable—a word that shares its origin with the word "miser"—in his heart and poor in spirit. Never satisfied, nothing seems to make him happy.

Contrast him with the man who works hard every day—including half days on Saturday for the overtime pay—and barely makes ends meet, despite living in a small, tidy home in a neighborhood that has seen better days, a car that makes funny noises parked out front. But he is wealthy. Life is good. He wishes some business decisions had turned out better, but he has a roof over his head and his family is fed and happy.

How can the man with so much be poor and the man with so little be rich? The difference is simple. One man is grateful for nothing. The other sees blessings everywhere. What is the secret to true wealth? A wealth that can never be taken away on the ups and downs of the stock market and business cycle? Gratitude.

May the righteous be glad and rejoice before God;
may they be happy and joyful.

PSALM 68:3

THE 10 PERCENT CLUB

Ten were healed. Only one returned to say thank you to the miracle worker. Does that percentage, only 10 percent, represent those in everyday life who stop to notice and express thanks for the miracles and ordinary blessings bestowed on them? Maybe. But this Scripture passage (Luke 17:11-19) is not about percentages. It's not about numbers—though it is about a number. The number one. The one Samaritan leper who expressed the gratitude of his heart.

Are you numbered with the 10 percent? Are you a kindred spirit with the one who gave thanks? Are you a person who sees miracles and blessings, or who wonders why things never go your way? Join an elite—though not exclusive—group. The 10 percent, the one who savors God's goodness and shouts out praise as a result.

One of them, when he saw he was healed, came back,
praising God in a loud voice. He threw himself at Jesus'
feet and thanked him—and he was a Samaritan.

LUKE 17:15-16

SAY THANKS

Everyone wants to feel appreciated. How do you feel when it seems your contributions at home, at work, or in a church or civic group are taken for granted? Just as importantly, how well do you say thank you to those who make a difference in your life? Colleagues? Friends? Family members? Mentors?

Paul began and ended all his New Testament letters by expressing his gratitude for the co-laborers who helped him spread the gospel of Jesus Christ. One letter, Philemon, is a very practical epistle written to a church leader. He wrote to Philemon, "I always thank my God as I remember you in my prayers, because I hear about your faith in the Lord Jesus and your love for all the saints" (verses 4-5). Paul knew to express appreciation to his fellow workers meaningfully and often.

To whom can you say thanks today? And how would your thank-you be most effective? Do you need to write an extended letter, purchase a meaningful gift, or make a special visit? Ask God to give you a spirit of gratitude—and the ability to express it well.

I thank God… as night and day
I constantly remember you in my prayers.

2 Timothy 1:3

IN THE FIERY FURNACE

In the biblical story of Shadrach, Meshach, and Abednego—three young men abducted into Babylonia during King Nebuchadnezzar's reign—we literally see grace under fire. (Look up Daniel 3 for the story.) The three young men refused to bow to any idol or serve any god other than the God of their fathers. When the king decreed that anyone who would not bow to an idol would be thrown into a furnace, Shadrach, Meshach, and Abednego stayed true to their principles. And the king had them bound and dragged into a fiery furnace. Amazingly, the three emerged from the furnace not only unscathed, but without even the smell of smoke on them.

They believed that God would rescue them from the flames. But just as importantly, they determined, even if He did not, they would not bow down to an idol. They had faith in God and faithfulness to Him. One tends to feed the other. Maybe you aren't facing a fiery furnace today, but you probably have your own tests of faith. If you cultivate faithfulness like Shadrach, Meshach, and Abednego's, your faith will grow. And you just might witness the impossible.

When you walk through the fire, you will not
be scorched, nor will the flame burn you.

Isaiah 43:2 nasb

PULLING THROUGH

His football career was legendary. He played for one of the most tradition-rich high schools in the state and even the nation. Even before his first college game, he ended up pictured on the front of a Wheaties box. He was a two-time All-American for Ohio State and went on to a long, award-filled NFL career, even overcoming a broken neck to extend his playing days.

But the biggest challenge of his life came when doctors diagnosed his wife with an aggressive malignant cancer. With the same passion he showed on the football field, he prayed and stood by his wife—leaving professional football for a year to be by her side. When she lost her hair to chemotherapy, he went with his two children to the barber so that all members of the family had shaven heads in a display of team solidarity. With faith and determination, the family pulled together as Mom pulled through for more than a decade before finally succumbing to the disease.

Life will very often call for us to respond with strength and perseverance. Fortunately, when we put our faith in God, He can supply all the strength we need.

Everything is possible for one who believes.

MARK 9:23

THE ARMOR OF GOD

Among people of faith, there is some variation in doctrine about spiritual warfare. Some see demons in everything. Others have more or less eliminated a personal devil from the equation of their spiritual practice. While we can go astray by devoting too much thought and care to Satan, the Bible does tell us that we must be on our guard against spiritual attacks.

Fortunately, we are never in the battle alone. God always arms us with His strength and enables us to defeat temptation and assaults on our Christian walk. In Ephesians 6, Paul wrote for us to take up the armor of God, including the shield of faith and the sword of the Spirit. We can deflect the attacks that would wound our souls by diligently nurturing our faith in God.

Our struggle is not against flesh and blood, but against the rulers, against the authorities, against the powers of this dark world and against the spiritual forces of evil in the heavenly realms.

EPHESIANS 6:12

RICHES OF GRACE

Did you know God favors you? Not because you are the smartest, not because you have lots of talents, not because you do many good deeds. No, God favors you out of His deep, abiding love for you, a love that is not contingent upon any effort you put forth.

Here are some aspects of grace that just might be what you need to hear today:

Grace provides the gift of salvation, a gift that can't be earned. Paul wrote, "For it is by grace you have been saved, through faith—and this not from yourselves, it is the gift of God—not by works, so that no one can boast" (Ephesians 2:8-9).

Grace is available to us when we are weak. Paul wrote, "Therefore I will boast all the more gladly about my weaknesses, so that Christ's power may rest on me" (2 Corinthians 12:9).

Grace is sufficient for absolutely any need we have—whether health, finances, relationships, temptations, or any other need. Paul wrote, "My grace is sufficient for you" (2 Corinthians 12:9).

Whatever need you have in your life today, be assured, God is on your side. He is ready and able to help you as you respond to Him with faith.

In him we have redemption through his blood, the forgiveness of sins, in accordance with the riches of God's grace.

Ephesians 1:7

DO WE REALLY
HAVE A CHOICE?

For centuries, people have debated what makes us who we are—are we born the way we are, or do we become this way through the things that happen to us? Though our genes and life experiences have a huge impact on us, aren't you glad there is a miraculous, powerful God who is able to change even the most stubborn, damaged, sinful heart? Paul went so far as to write, "Therefore, if anyone is in Christ, he is a new creation; old things have passed away; behold, all things have become new" (2 Corinthians 5:17 NKJV).

But you don't understand how I've been brought up. You don't know the mistakes I've made. You don't understand how hard it is for me to break certain negative patterns.

With grace, with faith, with the help of godly friends, you can say along with Paul: "Forgetting what is behind and straining toward what is ahead, I press on toward the goal to win the prize for which God has called me heavenward in Christ Jesus" (Philippians 3:13-14). Because of His forgiving, life-changing power, God's ultimate concern with your life is not where you've been, but where you are going.

We were therefore buried with him through baptism into death in order that, just as Christ was raised from the dead through the glory of the Father, we too may live a new life.

ROMANS 6:4

FAITH AND TRUST

We operate by faith every day. When we sit on a chair, we trust that it will hold us. When we get behind the wheel of our car, we put faith in the brakes to work. We accelerate after a green light, believing cross traffic will stop for reds. We drink bottled water because we believe it has been purified and is safe. Without thinking or questioning, we act as if the objects and many of the circumstances in our lives will come through for us, will be safe for us, because they almost always have.

Putting trust in an invisible God is different and can be a scarier proposition. We can't physically see Him the way we see a chair or a car or the clarity of water or the smiles on neighbors' faces. But when we seek to know Him, we can know His character. And we find that He will always come through for us. With that thought firmly in our minds, we can trust Him.

Lord, help me to know You and overcome any doubts. I want to trust You more than anything. Amen.

> *May your whole spirit, soul and body be kept*
> *blameless at the coming of our Lord Jesus Christ.*
> *The one who calls you is faithful, and he will do it.*
>
> 1 Thessalonians 5:23-24

WORRY AND FAITH

Fear and faith are diametrically opposed. When we live in fear, it erodes our faith in God. When worries creep in and dominate our thinking, we start to feel far from God.

How can we overcome the force of worry and choose faith instead? One simple discipline that will help is choosing to let problems and worries drive you to God instead of away from Him. Instead of mulling incessantly over the mortgage payment, pray and thank God for His provision. When someone you love is sick, meditate on verses that celebrate God as a healer. If work pressures are constantly gnawing at you, commit your work to God and begin each day with prayer.

The only way to grow spiritually is to bring more and more of ourselves to our relationship with God. Don't suppress or deny your fears. Let them lead you to God.

I pray that out of his glorious riches he may strengthen you with power through his Spirit in your inner being, so that Christ may dwell in your hearts through faith.

Ephesians 3:16-17

THE WISE STILL SEEK

What does the world seek in life? Many seek riches. Others chase fame. Still others race after success. Some pursue pleasure.

Who were these magi of the East? We don't know a lot about them, not even how many there were, but we do know that they were men of goodwill who wanted to discover spiritual truth. The cost of their journey and the gifts they carried would have been staggering, so they weren't in this for personal gain. Their first concern wasn't their own safety or they would have let Herod know the location of the child on their return home. If it was comfort they sought, they would have never begun the journey in the first place.

No, these men had sincere hearts. They knew there was something greater than they already knew and they were willing to pay the cost to discover it. In the same way, if we are wise, we still seek to know God in His fullness today. And that trip begins with a visit to a manger.

Where is the one who has been born king of the Jews?
We saw his star when it rose and have come to worship him.

MATTHEW 2:2

KEEP GOING

During a long race, it's easy to get discouraged. But what most runners know is that being familiar with the course helps to keep up momentum and motivation. When you know what to expect, you're able to pace yourself and not become discouraged when the road seems endless.

God doesn't map out for us the exact course of our lives. But there are some things we can know without a shadow of a doubt. We know troubles will come. We know that God will never abandon us. We know that He has good plans for us. And we know that He will ultimately overcome evil in the world. That knowledge and faith helps us persevere when the going gets tough and the race gets long.

God, give me greater confidence in You so that I might persevere in the race of life. Amen.

> *Let us draw near to God with a sincere heart and with the*
> *full assurance that faith brings, having our hearts*
> *sprinkled to cleanse us from a guilty conscience*
> *and having our bodies washed with pure water.*
>
> HEBREWS 10:22

To learn more about Harvest House books and
to read sample chapters, visit our website:

www.harvesthousepublishers.com

HARVEST HOUSE PUBLISHERS
EUGENE, OREGON